Insider's Guide to

ASSISTED LIVING

What You Really Need to Know
Before You Sign A Contract

Molly Shomer, M.S., M.S.S.W., PGCM

Aeltern Press • Dallas, TX

Inquiries should be addressed to:

AELTERN PRESS

Box 700291 • Dallas, Texas 75370

VOICE: (972) 395-7823 • FAX: (972) 395-7164 • *www.eldercareteam.com*

Publisher's Cataloging-in-Publication Data

Shomer, Molly

Insider's guide to assisted living: what you really need to know before you sign a contract / Molly Shomer. — 1st ed. — Dallas, TX : Aeltern Press, 2005, c2004.

p. ; cm.

ISBN: 0-97492-755-4

1. Older people—Care—Decision making. 2. Older people—Care—United States—Evaluation. 3. Older people—Care—United States—Costs. 4. Older people—Housing—United States—Evaluation. 5. Older people—Housing—United States—Costs. 6. Nursing homes—United States—Evaluation. 7. Old age homes—United States—Evaluation. 8. Congregate housing—United States—Evaluation

I. Title

HD7287.92.U6 S56 2005
362.1/6/0973—dc22   0501

Cover and Interior Design © TLC Graphics, www.TLCGraphics.com

Printed in the United States of America

DEDICATION

This book is dedicated to my father, George Erdmann, who wanted so desperately to make it into assisted living, and to my mother Susanne Erdmann, who gave us the gift of one more year before she departed to join him forever.

And to all the seniors, daughters and sons, husbands and wives, in-laws and outlaws who have so enriched my life by allowing me to be a part of yours. I am proud to have been permitted to know each and every one of you.

You have all taught me well.

Table of Contents

Preface

It's downright amazing to look back at the changes that our parents have seen in their lifetimes. During the Great Depression, times were tough and life expectancy for our parents' parents averaged less than 65 years. There was no such thing as health insurance. My own grandfather, a physician in Davenport, Iowa, really did accept chickens from his patients as payment in the 1930s. And he was glad to get them, too.

During that era, wives and mothers worked mostly at home. They cared for their elderly and infirm relatives at home, too. They didn't have the medical technology that we have today, and their elderly loved ones rarely needed care for more than a few years.

That's all changed in a matter of a little more than two generations. With health insurance, most of us have adequate medical care. The U.S. Census reveals that life expectancy has increased to the point that, if you live to see age 65, you'll probably live to see 85. There are now so many centenarians (age 100 and older) that you have to request congratulations from the President many months in advance of the 100th birthday in order to get a card in time. Newspapers and television shows rarely take note any more.

But something else has changed, too. Wives and mothers aren't at home any more to take care of aging loved ones. Medicare may pay the medical bills, but families aren't always available to move in to help, or to take an older person into their own homes. Just about everyone is working full-time, and the daughter who was once at home to care for her mother is now trying to juggle a job and her own children.

Many families are separated by distance, as adult children move away to pursue their own lives and careers and leave the "old folks" behind at home.

More and more older people are on their own in their homes as they struggle with illness, forgetfulness, and the general frailties of aging bodies.

Until recently the only alternative was to make home care work, or move an aging person into a nursing home. Most seniors, of course, chose to make do at home with whatever help they could hire or with the help of overstretched daughters and sons.

Then, about a decade ago, personal care homes and assisted living residences began to make an appearance. For many of those who could afford it, moving to a place with regular meals and regular attention made all the difference in their quality of life.

In 2001, the Assisted Living Federation, a private industry group, reported that almost one million seniors were living in assisted living facilities all over the country, and the numbers continue to grow.

Today, just about everyone knows something about assisted living. But everyone seems to have a different idea about what it is, and what it can do to enhance the lives of seniors.

Most of the public's information still comes from the marketing efforts of the large assisted living chains. And what you see in a marketing brochure isn't necessarily what you get.

Lately, I spend quite a bit of my time helping families and seniors who either want to look into assisted living, or who aren't particularly happy with the residence they have already chosen. Often, both groups share the same misconceptions about what assisted living is and what it can do.

I sincerely hope that the information in this book will give you the "insider" knowledge you need to make a really informed decision about any assisted living facility that you might be evaluating - even if you already live there.

Introduction

In August, 2001, the U.S. Senate Special Committee on Aging called together a group of assisted living providers, healthcare organizations, regulatory agencies, and advocacy groups. Their charge was to develop guidelines for improving assisted living care. In April 2003, the Assisted Living Workgroup released its preliminary findings.

Remarkably, despite almost 18 months of effort, the workgroup was unable to agree even on their first priority – a single definition of what, exactly, assisted living *is*.

So it isn't so surprising that families are still confused, too. Just what *is* Assisted Living? And, maybe even more importantly, what is Assisted Living *not?*

What Assisted Living *Is Not*

Assisted living is not, and was never designed to be, a residential option for people who need intensive medical care, continuous around-the-clock supervision, or who are bedridden or unable to move around on their own.

If a potential resident needs help to eat, falls frequently, needs to have a call bell answered fast and often in order to be safe, or needs the daily care of medical professionals, then assisted living isn't going to be the best choice for her.

Misunderstandings about what assisted living can offer are the biggest cause of conflicts between residences and families. It is important that family members understand the limitations of assisted living before they start to look for a care residence.

What Assisted Living *Is*

Assisted living is designed to be a residential choice for people who want and need help with some of the basic activities that we all need to do every day. These activities primarily consist of personal care (bathing, dressing, grooming), meal preparation, and keeping track of medications. Sometimes, the resident just needs some reminders and coaching, and sometimes real hands-on help is needed.

Rather than receive this help in their own homes, people who choose to live in an assisted living facility have chosen a "congregate" (group) living environment. They usually have one or two primary reasons for choosing this kind of living: cost is considerably less than the cost of either homecare or a nursing home, and the social opportunities are much greater than what might be available at either place.

In general, assisted living is designed to offer a "social" rather than a "medical" living environment. Residents aren't seriously ill, and they don't move to assisted living to receive medical care. They may need some help and guidance with daily activities, including some health care needs. But they are first and foremost unique individuals who want to continue living as independently, and with as much dignity, as possible.

CHAPTER ONE

First Things First

Why are you thinking about assisted living for yourself or a loved one?

Before you jump to answer, have you taken a detailed look at what your needs really are? If you haven't, there's a good chance you're going to be disappointed with the facility you choose.

■   ■   ■

Janet came to the decision that her Uncle Thomas needed to move to assisted living. When she visited from her home in London, England, she could see that Parkinson's Disease and a small stroke were making it difficult for him to get around. Neighbors reported that the volunteer fire department had been by several times to get him up off the floor.

Thomas had no other family, except for Janet, who lives abroad. So she located a nice-looking assisted living residence nearby with an "aging in place" philosophy. She also found a new doctor who would do the medical paperwork necessary so that Thomas could move in.

This doctor was seeing Thomas for the first time, and he relied heavily on what Janet told him, since her uncle wasn't much of

1

a talker. Janet didn't know much about Parkinson's. She did know that Uncle Thomas could no longer get out of bed by himself and that he was sleeping in his electric recliner. She knew he coughed a lot when he drank or if food went down wrong. She was sure that, if he stopped eating and drinking in his recliner, the choking would stop. Unfortunately, neither Janet nor Thomas told the doctor about either of these problems. Even more unfortunately, the doctor seemed to be in a bit of a rush and didn't ask a lot of questions.

The assisted living residence reviewed the doctor's paperwork and approved Thomas. Janet got him moved in and settled, and then she returned to England. Less than three months later, Janet got a call from the manager of Thomas' new residence. Thomas had been sent to the hospital with pneumonia. They wouldn't be able to take him back because Thomas now needed help from two people to get out of his chair, and he needed to be fed. Thomas' Parkinson's Disease had progressed to the point that he needed nursing care. He wouldn't be able to "age in place," at that particular residence.

■   ■   ■

Could you be underestimating the amount of help your elder really needs? Have you considered that, even though he's doing fairly well today, your elder, like Thomas, may have a progressive illness that will eventually be very debilitating?

Or, could you be *overestimating* the amount of care your elder really needs? Are you looking for assisted living, when truly all your elder might need to remain independent is some help with transportation or a home-delivered meal? In that case, maybe a less structured retirement apartment would be a better answer. For that matter, a gift certificate for taxi rides might even do the trick.

■   ■   ■

My mother actually wanted to move out of her house and into an assisted living residence because she didn't want to cook and clean any more. She said she'd been doing that for 50 years, and she was done with it. So we visited a few places. All the people seemed to be so much older and sicker than my mother was, and so many of them were confused. She got really depressed.

Then we stumbled on The Gardens. She has her own apartment. She can cook for herself, or go to the dining room for meals. They clean her apartment every week. The van goes somewhere every day. She says she wishes they had known about this place while my father was still alive.

— Monique

■ ■ ■

Are you looking at this kind of living alternative because of social opportunities you think would be good for your loved one? If your elder has always been painfully shy, has always avoided groups, and prefers solitary pursuits, moving him to a large group living situation isn't going to change his personality. In fact, it could turn out to be cruel and intolerable for him.

On the other hand, maybe a small and cozy residential home with only one or two other residents might be absolutely ideal.

■ ■ ■

Mrs. Albert, a German war bride, once spoke excellent English. Now Alzheimer's Disease is stealing her English away, and she speaks mostly in German. Her family looked high and low for an Alzheimer's home where someone would be able to communicate with her. Word of mouth finally sent them to a neighborhood care home where the owner speaks a little German. Mrs. Albert thinks the homeowner is her sister. She's content there.

■ ■ ■

Can you afford it? If it's a financial stretch now, what will happen when needs increase, the rates go up, and more expensive medications are prescribed? Even if the resident's needs don't increase in the short term, will expected annual rate raises be a hardship?

The absolute first-things-first step is a complete and accurate assessment:

Physical Needs – What kind of help is necessary now, and what changes can you reasonably expect in the future?

Financial Realities – How much is available now to pay for care, and how long will the money last?

Emotional Issues – Are there psychiatric or behavioral problems that need to be addressed?

Social Concerns – Are there strong ties to a group or place that need to be maintained? Is the resident-to-be outgoing or shy? Is family nearby, or far away?

All these things need to be carefully analyzed. If you don't feel confident that you can do this on your own, you'll get more than your money's worth if you bring in a geriatric specialist to help with this step. If you need help locating a qualified geriatric professional, one excellent resource is the National Association of Professional Geriatric Care Managers. Their website at www.caremanager.org is a good place to start.

Your First Visits

Visit as many residences as you can which fit the profile of the needs that you put together from the short assessment you just completed. Don't eliminate those that are several miles away. Although it is best to find a quality residence that's close enough to visit frequently, closeness isn't everything.

Remember that your elder has to live there 24 hours a day. You'll be visiting for short periods of time. If the best place is the farthest away, it might still be the best choice.

Don't eliminate the older facilities, either. The latest in architecture and decor are designed primarily to appeal to families. Residents care more about how pleasant it might be to actually live there.

Take the guided tour and ask the questions that are important to you. Use your eyes, your ears, your nose, and your taste buds if you're invited to have a meal (you probably will be).

If you'll be looking at several places, take along your camera. Pictures will help you remember which facility was which as you review your notes. Be aware, though, that most residences will ask you to respect their residents' privacy by not taking pictures of individuals.

Visit as many facilities as possible so you can start the narrowing-down process. Take "The Tour" to get your most basic questions answered.

Then Go Back to the Best

Pick out what seem to the best two or three. Go back at a different day and time – without an appointment, if possible. If you can, find an out-of-the way place to sit and watch how the residents and staff interact. Visit with someone who lives there (away from the front desk) about what they like or don't like. If you run into visiting families, ask them, too.

Are the activities listed on the monthly calendar actually happening? If it's the weekend, is anything at *all* going on? Do there seem to be enough staff members available? Do they look and behave as if they like the people they work with at the facility?

If you run into a manager, and the manager seems to be uncomfortable leaving you on your own, ask yourself, "why?"

If possible, do this at least two or three times, varying your days and times. By now you should know whether this is "The Place" for your loved one.

Twice is nice, three times is better when you're making a long-term residential choice. Try to leave your emotions at home on at least the first two visits. Remember, too, that there's no such thing as perfection in this world.

Review the Reviews

If it hasn't already been offered (and it's a very good sign if it was) ask for a copy of the most recent state inspection report (most states regularly check to make sure basic regulations are being followed). If there were no "deficiencies" reported, then you know that this facility has met at least the *minimum* standards required by the state.

If there were "deficiencies," what were they, and have they been corrected? Just because a residence might have had a deficiency is no reason to disqualify it. Deficiencies can range from minor paperwork problems to serious injury to one or more residents – and everything in between. If the deficiency wasn't terribly significant, didn't harm anyone, and has been corrected, then just take it under advisement.

On the other hand, if you see that the residence has had problems with sanitation, medications, or actual harm to any of the residents, then be prepared to cross it off your list.

You can also call the "Long Term Care Ombudsman," and ask for a report about any complaints that have been made. Remember, though, just because there has been a complaint doesn't mean that the residence is poor quality. Many complaints are either very minor or truly aren't justified. The Ombudsman can give you an idea of how frequent complaints have been, and how they were resolved. You can locate your local Ombudsman by calling your state "Oversight Agency" listed in Appendix II.

OK – You're Finished

Rank your choices from best to worst, make your choice, sign the contract and move in...

...Whoa! Take a step back. There's a bit more to do.

You've shopped around, you've done your due diligence, and you've made your decision. You visited several times. You talked with residents and their families, and you sampled the meals. You've carefully read over the brochures and other printed materials that describe what they offer. You've even measured the room. You've found what looks like the right assisted living residence. Now all that's left is to do the paperwork and move in. Right?

No! Before you make that appointment to go in and sign on the dotted line, take the time to go over the contract. If you have questions or concerns, the time to get answers is *before* you sign. The Resident Contract is a binding legal document. As with any other legal document, it's critically important to know what you're signing, and what it means.

The contract you're about to sign sets the legal ground rules for where you or your elder will live, what you will pay, what services you will receive, and when the facility can demand that you move out. This isn't a document to be taken lightly.

If you're like most people who shop for an assisted living residence, you've gathered a lot of marketing materials. You've spent hours looking over the photographs, the floor plans, the menus and the list of "amenities."

Marketing materials have been known to promise a whole lot more than they can actually deliver. It's too bad that marketing materials aren't legally binding. If you've chosen a facility on the basis of what you saw in a colorful brochure, you would be smart to verify everything that you think you will be receiving. Check for each amenity in the contract. If it is not in the contract, then you *have* no guarantees.

When you were looking around, the brochure or the person giving you the tour may have assured you that your elder could "age in place," in their facility. Unless they also offer skilled nursing services, look closely at that "aging in place" promise.

One of the bigger misunderstandings about assisted living is the idea that an older resident should be able to live out the rest of his or her life there, no matter what the medical or long term care needs might be. By the very nature of getting older, a person who lives a long, long time will inevitably become frail. When someone progresses from needing help ("assistance") to needing total care, then an assisted living facility is no longer the right place for that person to be living.

In fact, unless you hire supplemental private caregivers, it might be against state regulations for an assisted living facility to provide care to a resident who is bed-bound, who has a catheter, who needs a tube to be fed, who has behavioral problems, or who needs constant care.

When you were looking at facilities, did the person giving you the tour offer to give you a copy of the contract to look over? Probably not. This doesn't necessarily indicate a problem. After all, when you shop for a house or an apartment, you aren't offered a copy of the contract until you express interest in renting or buying.

If you didn't think to ask for a copy of the contract when you were visiting, then ask to see a copy now, before you make an appointment to actually sign. The manager or marketing representative shouldn't hesitate to give you a copy. He or she should encourage you to review it carefully and make note of any questions.

If the manager or administrator won't let you take a copy of the contract out of the building before you actually come in to sign, then run, run, run and don't come back! You have good reason to be afraid!

You should also get copies of the Resident Handbook, Resident "Rights and Responsibilities," and any other document that outlines who is responsible for what. Many contracts refer to the "Residents' Handbook" or other documents, and they will incorporate the contents of these publications, making them part of the contract.

Read everything carefully!
Twice!

If you can, have an attorney read everything over carefully, too. This may be easier said than done – there aren't many attorneys who are familiar with assisted living and the "nitty-gritty" of what it actually is.

An Elder Law attorney should be well-versed in Medicaid and estate planning, but isn't likely to know much about assisted living leases and contracts. He or she probably hasn't spent much time inside an actual assisted living residence.

A real estate or contract law specialist will often be equally in the dark. Before you ask an attorney to review your documents, make sure that he or she has some expertise and understands the concept of assisted living.

When you actually meet with the owner or the administrator of your chosen residence to sign the contract, there shouldn't be any documents offered for your signature that you haven't had a chance to read and understand well in advance.

There are things that won't be in the contract, but you should grab your opportunity and discuss them at length before you make a commitment. Once you have signed a contract, it's too late.

One or more attorneys who represent the facility's owner probably wrote the assisted living contract. If the residence you are looking at is part of a chain, then the contract is probably one that the "home office" uses for all of the residences it owns.

If so, there isn't much chance that you'll be able to change the terms of the contract you're being asked to sign. Like most real estate leases, the assisted living contract is hardly ever one where the consumer can negotiate special terms.

Therefore, it is very important that you understand up front what you're agreeing to. If you aren't comfortable with the terms and conditions of the contract, usually your only option is to look elsewhere, or accept what you can't change.

At least, if you've read and understood the contract, you'll know where you're agreeing to compromise, if in fact you *are* compromising. You won't be happy to find out later that you've compromised without knowing it.

While you're reading, try to keep in mind that, by necessity, congregate (group) living requires some regimentation. It isn't possible for every resident to have complete freedom of choice when living in a group setting.

If you're considering a small "board and care" home, then the contract may be fairly simple – somewhere between a handshake and one or two pages. I don't recommend a handshake and a verbal understanding. This kind of "gentleman's agreement," while friendly, leaves far too much to chance and good will.

Because board and care homes are usually small and privately owned, there may be more opportunity to negotiate than you might find with contracts used by the larger facilities.

Whether you're looking at just a few paragraphs, or a complex, multi-page corporate document, there are a lot of things to look for, and a lot of questions to ask. Many of your questions will be answered in the documents you are about to sign. Others won't, and you will have to rely on the answers you get when you ask questions.

Keep in mind that the verbal answers you get from an administrator or a marketing representative are NOT legally binding.

If you have serious concerns about something, and you would like to see it covered in writing, you have nothing to lose by asking to have it incorporated into the contract. But if you are not dealing directly with an owner, then there is probably not much chance that the contract can or will be changed.

If the person you are dealing with does offer to include or change something in the contract, be sure that person has the authority to make contract changes. In a large facility you may be talking to an employee who doesn't have the authority to alter legal documents.

Only you can decide what will be a "deal breaker" and what won't.

CHAPTER TWO

Might It Be Covered?

 If you plan on using long-term care insurance benefits to help pay for assisted living costs, pull out your policy well before you make a final residential selection. Does the plan cover assisted living?

Most long-term care insurance providers now routinely offer coverage for assisted living care. Some of the older plans may not.

If your policy covers skilled nursing care and has an "Alternate Plan of Care" benefit for care in another setting, check with the insurance company. What are their rules for covering assisted living?

■ What will be required so that the insured person can use this coverage?

_____

_____

_____

_____

■ Can you get approval from the insurance company for the particular facility you're looking at before you commit to moving in?

_____

_____

_____

■ What paperwork will the insurance company want from the facility, and what will they want from the resident's private physician?

_____

_____

_____

■ Will they want to have an interview with the prospective resident (the policyholder) before they certify that assisted living care is appropriate and necessary?

_____

_____

_____

■ If an interview or a particular kind of medical examination is required before benefits will be authorized, can you get this out of the way before you move forward?

_____

_____

_____

Have the insurance company send you any forms the doctor will have to fill out.

The policy should clearly state the plan's definition of assisted living, including licensing requirements, the minimum acceptable size of the facility, staffing requirements (particularly whether a registered nurse must be on staff), and the services the facility has to offer.

Gather all of the documents the insurance company will need, including a copy of the facility's license. Make arrangements to get these documents sent to the insurance company *before* you sign a lease (make sure you keep copies of everything you send). If there are any problems in using your insurance at the residence you are choosing then it is better to resolve them before you sign on the dotted line.

Clarify with the insurance company how and when they will pay claims.

Most assisted living facilities aren't willing to wait for insurance benefits to come in. They will want the insured resident to pay the rent and any other fees at the beginning of the month. They expect that the resident will then be reimbursed by the insurance company for whatever the covered amount is.

Long-term care insurance usually reimburses for care that has actually been provided. It won't pay in advance. So, the insured has to have enough funds available to pay for fees, deposits, and the first covered month in advance . . . in addition to however many days or months are in the "elimination period" (the deductible). The insured also must be able to pay in advance for the second covered month while waiting for the first month's reimbursement check.

And so on. The insured person (the beneficiary) will always be one to two months behind in receiving reimbursement.

Many families don't plan ahead for these upfront costs when they intend to use a long-term care policy.

CHAPTER THREE

The Legal Documents

Moving-in day isn't the best time to be looking at the "Resident Contract" for the first time. Until you read the actual lease/contract document, you may not realize that it isn't the only piece of paper you might need to read and think about. There may be two, three or even more documents that, together, make up the "Contract."

■ ■ ■

My brother, who is a lawyer, volunteered to look over the contract. I asked the marketing person for a copy and sent it to him. My brother called back to say he needed a copy of their "Handbook," because the contract said the rules in the Handbook were binding on all the residents, and violation of the rules were grounds for being kicked out.

First, I asked the director for a copy on her voicemail. She never called back. Then I drove over and asked for one in person. She told me they were "fresh out," and new copies hadn't come back from the printer. But the marketing director would call me in a couple of days when they came in.

I called again. No return call. I called the corporate office and a very nice woman said she would send one out that day. No Handbook.

After about ten days I finally decided if they were that hard to deal with before Mom even moved in, it could only get worse. So we eventually chose another place."

— Mark

- Exactly what documents actually make up the contract at the residence you're considering?

_____

_____

_____

- Does the contract stand alone, or does it make reference to a "Resident Handbook" or other documents?

_____

_____

_____

- Does the contract say that the contents of those other documents are incorporated into, or are part of, the contract?

_____

_____

_____

- If the Handbook, "Resident Behavior Policy," or another document is "part" of the contract, does the contract say these other documents can be changed or revised by the facility at any time?

_____

_____

_____

When you're reading the contract, if you see that the facility can change or amend any part of it "as appropriate," or "as necessary," this means that they can change it whenever they wish. What it amounts to is that the residence might be able to change the contract at any time, and if you've signed it, you'll have no choice but to accept their changes without warning.

CHAPTER FOUR

Who's Really Financially Responsible?

The simple fact is that many of the people who move into assisted living are beginning to have some problems with memory and/or money management. So, most facilities are hesitant to accept a resident without a responsible party as a backup. The responsible party is required to *personally* guarantee that all rent and fees will be promptly and correctly paid.

If you aren't prepared to accept this responsibility DO NOT sign any document that will commit you to do so.

Understand, though, that if you refuse, the number of residences you may then be able to choose from might be severely limited.

■　■　■

When we moved Dad in he was having some trouble moving around, but there was nothing wrong with his mind. He was keeping up with his personal business and bills just fine, and he had more than enough to be able to afford the place. So I didn't pay much attention when I signed their "Responsible

Party" form – there must have been a hundred papers to go through that day.

Then Dad got mad at them about something or other and he wouldn't pay the monthly bill. They came to me for it. I was laid off a while ago, and we don't have $2,500 a month for Dad to stay there. It got really ugly between my father and me. Dad finally wrote the check, but now I'm always worried that he'll do it again. He won't give me the checkbook, and I can't take it away from him.

— Joe

■   ■   ■

If you have been given the resident's Power of Attorney, and you're signing documents on the resident's behalf, be sure and check with an attorney for instructions on how to sign these kinds of documents so that you don't obligate your own funds. There is often very specific wording an attorney will suggest you use.

When in doubt, have all the documents reviewed by an attorney before you, or your elder, sign them.

CHAPTER FIVE

Where's My Room?

 It doesn't much matter whether we are 3 or 103 years old, we all need to know where our place is, and that our place will be there the way we left it. It's no different in supportive living.

No matter if you're looking at the middle bedroom in a small personal care home, or the two-bedroom suite in a high-rise with over 100 apartments, you want to know that the place you have chosen is the place you are getting. You also want to know how, and under what circumstances, you might later be asked to move to another room or apartment.

■ How is the apartment or room that you have chosen identified on the lease agreement? What is the exact apartment number?

_____

_____

_____

_____

- Is it absolutely clear on the lease that your elder will be living in the apartment or room that you have chosen?

_____

_____

- What is the facility's policy on relocating or moving residents within the facility? Can a resident be moved to another apartment or room without consent?

_____

_____

■　■　■

I was looking for a two-bedroom apartment since my in-laws wanted to live together, but not that together. Assisted living apartments that large are scarce, and there weren't any available. The manager was very eager to help and he showed me a vacant one-bedroom apartment. Next door was a studio apartment with someone living in it. He said they would move the lady living next door to a different studio apartment, and they would cut a door between the two apartments to make a large suite. This sounded like a great idea for everyone except the poor lady living next door. Apparently no one was going to ask her how she felt about this plan.

— Linda

■　■　■

Roommates

Although it generally costs less than care in a nursing home, supportive living isn't cheap. In order to economize, or for social reasons, some people choose to share a room with a roommate.

Having a roommate is often quite successful. There is someone to talk to, eat with, and go to activities with. There is another person to help keep a slightly confused or forgetful resident on track. It's not so lonely.

Of course, it doesn't always work out that way. Roommates can snore. They can be nosy and hard to get along with.

If your prospective resident is planning on sharing a room, look for answers to these questions before you make a commitment:

- If a resident has agreed to share a room or apartment with a roommate, what happens if they aren't compatible? Will both be consulted about any changes?

  _____

  _____

  _____

- If a roommate leaves the facility, will the resident staying on be consulted before being assigned another roommate?

  _____

  _____

- If a roommate leaves, will the remaining resident be charged the private room rate until a new roommate moves in?

  _____

  _____

  _____

Furnishings

When you were touring and looking at possibilities, you might have seen "model" apartments. If you were looking at a small residential home, you might have seen a room where someone was still residing.

Especially if you looked at a room that was furnished when you saw it, check the contract to see what furniture and amenities are included. Most likely the resident will be expected to bring personal items to furnish the room.

■ If the prospective resident is moving from a distance and has to wait until the moving truck brings furniture from a previous residence, does the new facility have furniture that can be "borrowed" for a short time until the truck arrives?

_____

_____

■ What amenities will be provided in the apartment or room? Are the window treatments included, or will the resident need to cover the windows?

_____

_____

■ Will it be necessary to bring a personal shower curtain?

_____

_____

■ If the resident will need to use a bath seat or bench in the tub or shower, and it is not built in, is one provided?

_____

_____

■ Will there be a refrigerator?

_____

_____

■ Will there be a microwave?

_____

_____

■ Is there access to cable television? If it isn't already installed, would the resident be permitted to have it installed?

_____

_____

■ What cable, phone, Internet or other services does the facility use, if any? What is the monthly cost for these various services?

_____

_____

_____

■ If your elder likes to use the Internet, would an extra, dedicated phone line be permitted?

_____

_____

- What is *not* permitted in the apartment? If there is no specific list of prohibited items, how about an electric coffeepot or an iron? What about other electrical appliances?

  _____

  _____

  _____

- If this is a facility or wing that is dedicated to Alzheimer's/ dementia, will the resident be permitted to have a private telephone and television? What about a radio? A VCR?*

  _____

  _____

  _____

*If you're looking at a residence devoted to dementia care, you'll probably be discouraged from bringing items like a VCR. Electronics – even televisions – are difficult enough to program and to use when cognitive skills are relatively good. They are unbelievably frustrating for someone who is confused.

Individuals with dementia often lose interest in television, and it can become a source of anxiety, as well. Although it isn't likely you'll see anything about it in the contract itself, don't be surprised or offended if you're asked not to bring these items.

Visitors

Moving from a home to a small room or apartment means many losses. One loss that tends to be overlooked is the spare room, the pull-out bed in the den, or the couch in the living room – the place where guests always stayed.

So, does this mean that the grandkids will never again be able to sleep over at Grammy's? Probably. This is an assisted living residence for older adults. Children aren't usually permitted to stay overnight. They should be welcome to visit and stay for a meal, though.

When adults visit from out of town, will they have to find a hotel room, even if they would be quite content to sleep on the day bed for one night? Sometimes things can be more flexible for adults.

- Will the resident be permitted to have guests stay in their room or apartment?

  _____

  _____

- Is there a maximum length of time a guest may stay?

  _____

  _____

- Is there another room in the facility that can be used by guests?

  _____

  _____

- What are the additional charges for guests, if any?

  _____

  _____

Other Companionship

Just because a person has gotten older, and may even need some assistance now and then, it doesn't mean that her emotional needs are declining, too. Many older people continue relationships that they developed before they moved to a care residence. Many make new friends. Some of these friendships blossom and grow.

Small residential homes don't have the population that larger facilities have, but deeply caring relationships can happen between two people anywhere.

Assuming that both people are competent to make this kind of choice, and no one is being forced:

- What are the rules if a resident should want to live with someone other than a spouse in his private room or apartment?

_____

_____

- Will there be objections to a resident sharing a private room or apartment with someone of the opposite sex?

_____

_____

- What are the additional charges for room, board, and services for a second occupant?

_____

_____

So How Much Will All This Cost?

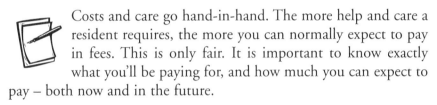 Costs and care go hand-in-hand. The more help and care a resident requires, the more you can normally expect to pay in fees. This is only fair. It is important to know exactly what you'll be paying for, and how much you can expect to pay – both now and in the future.

Study your contract carefully. The basic monthly rent for a room will be clearly stated. But, as they say, the Devil is in the details, and there may be other fees and charges that are harder to decipher.

It is especially dangerous to figure your budget down to the last dollar so that your older loved one can move into a particular residence. There will always be annual rent increases. Inevitably, your costs will rise as care needs increase. If you are working close to the financial edge when your elder first moves in, you may soon find yourself having to look for a less expensive alternative.

A surprisingly large number of facilities charge a flat rate for room, board, and all services. Many, but not all, are the smaller residential homes. If this is the case with the place you are looking at, it will be an easy job to calculate how much more you will be paying over time, since usually only across-the-board rent increases come with lease renewals.

It is important to clearly understand what your contract says is included in the base rate, and what supplemental charges will be added on for "extra" services.

Most of the larger assisted living facilities will offer a package of services in their "base," or lowest, level of care. Any extra service translates into additional service fees. Usually, the base level will include three daily meals, weekly housekeeping, weekly flat linen service, and possibly, some activities and limited transportation.

If the facility you are looking at is brand new, it will be especially important to understand how and when rates and fees may be increased. A new facility will be full of empty rooms. Often, "fill-'er-up" rates are offered in order to attract residents quickly. These rates may be substantially less than the going rate in nearby facilities.

When the new facility is full, then rates may begin to climb. If there is no "cap" on the amount or percent that base rent and fees can climb every year, you can generally expect to be paying quite a bit more within 12 to 24 months.

- What is the base monthly rent?

  _____

  _____

  _____

- What other initial payments are required (deposit, application fee, assessment fee, move-in fee, utilities, pet deposit, parking fee, electric wheelchair/scooter deposit)?

  _____

  _____

  _____

■ Are any of these fees refundable?

_____

_____

■ How and when will fees be refunded?

_____

_____

■ Are refundable deposit fees placed in a trust account? If not, what is the guarantee that this money will be available if the facility is sold or closed?

_____

_____

_____

■ Is there a limit on the amount (dollars or percent) that the base room rate can be increased at the end of the contract period?

_____

_____

_____

■ How does the facility charge for services: Is everything included in the base rate with no extra charges? Is a "level" system in place? Does the facility assess "points" for every service provided?

_____

_____

_____

"Assessment fees" and "move-in" fees, in particular, are something to watch out for. In recent years there has been a building boom in the assisted living industry. The resulting large number of available apartments in some parts of the country has led to some pretty aggressive "price wars."

With the pressure growing to keep monthly rates down or lose business to the competition, facilities got creative in finding other ways to generate income. And so the "assessment" or "move-in" fee was born.

It's not unusual to see non-refundable entrance fees as high as $3,000 to $4,000, being charged for meeting with the resident for an "assessment," reviewing medical documents, setting up medical charts, and preparing a shadow box by the door with memorabilia provided by the family.

If you pro-rate this *non-refundable* amount over the 18 months that the average person lives in assisted living, you have an effective increase in the monthly rent of $166 to $222 per month. When the resident moves out for whatever reason, the facility keeps these fees.

Families do seem to be catching on to this, and if pressed, some facilities will "waive" the assessment or move-in fees. Don't hesitate to ask.

Figuring out how much all of this will really cost depends a lot on the answers you get to some of the questions posed in the following chapters.

CHAPTER SEVEN

Assessment & "Plan of Care"

 In order to know in advance what kind of help a new resident will need, an assisted living facility should require an "assessment" in advance of move-in. This assessment is a review of what the resident is able to do on his or her own, and what help will be needed on a predictable basis.

Most good facilities will want the assessment to be completed before the resident moves in. This is helpful, not only to confirm what kind of help their new resident will likely need, but because you'll know in advance approximately how much you'll have to pay for care in addition to the base rate.

Some facilities make the argument that a new resident needs a few weeks to adjust to the new living situation before an assessment would be fair and accurate.

Keep in mind that, if the assessment is postponed until the end of the first 30 days, any trial period will likely be over. You might then be committed by your contract to pay for a higher level of care than you anticipated.

- When is the first assessment of a resident's initial "level of care" needs scheduled?

  _____

  _____

- Who does the assessment? The administrator? The nurse? A team?

  _____

  _____

- What training or qualifications does this person or this team have to make this kind of an assessment?

  _____

  _____

- How often will the "level of care" be routinely reassessed throughout the time an individual lives at the facility?

  _____

  _____

If the residence you're considering uses a "point" system, ask for a copy of whatever system they use to assess points and keep track of how many have been used. This will give you an idea of how they figure their individual points, and what you will have to watch out for.

■　■　■

My mother is a "just-so" kind of a woman. She would keep the housekeeper busy every day, arranging and rearranging her little figurines and pictures, and hanging the towels in the bathroom so the monograms were perfectly centered.

They wanted to raise her level of care – an extra $300 a month – because the housekeeper was spending so much time with her. We showed her the new rate schedule and Mother quickly lost interest in how her dresser and towels looked.

— Shane

■　■　■

Sometimes, one of the harder things to figure out is just how much help a person really needs. A resident who isn't encouraged to be as independent as possible is likely to react in one of two ways:

1. he'll become angry or resentful about restrictions to his independence, or

2. she'll give up doing those things she is perfectly capable of doing, and eventually lose the ability to do them.

■ Are the resident and family members involved in the facility's decision about the level of care to be provided?

_____

_____

■ What is the procedure if the resident and family don't agree with the assessment?

_____

_____

_____

■ Is there a written "care plan" based on the needs assessment that you can read?

_____

_____

■ What happens if the resident has a brief illness and needs extra help only for a short period of time? Is there a definition of "short?"

_____

_____

_____

■ If the resident asks for unscheduled extra help, will any extra additional charges be discussed with the resident and the family before services are provided?

_____

_____

It is an unfortunate fact of life that costs for everything will go up. The base room and board rate should be fixed by the contract for at least 12 months. Any "fee schedule" published separately from the base rate should also be fixed for the same length of time. This doesn't mean that fees won't be added if the resident needs more assistance, but the cost of the fees for this assistance won't be raised for the duration. This way, you'll be able to anticipate fairly accurately how much your costs will rise if and when the resident needs more services.

■ When and why can rates or service fees be changed?

_____

_____

_____

- How much warning will you get when service fees are going to be raised?

  _____

  _____

  _____

- Who is notified when fees will change?

  _____

  _____

- How are these notices distributed?

  _____

  _____

■　■　■

They used to slip announcements under everyone's door. One old lady would wander down the hall and gather up everything that stuck out the littlest bit. For quite a while no one could figure out why the residents said they never got their messages. Although the fact is that half of them wouldn't have remembered the fliers anyway. We never got copies of anything while that was going on.

— Patricia

■　■　■

For one reason or another, a flyer under the door probably won't make it into the hands of a responsible family member. If someone other than the resident is managing the finances, it's very important that the resident not be the only person notified of important changes.

CHAPTER EIGHT

But I Need To Know What's Going On

 One reason that caregivers feel guilty about having a loved one in a residential facility is a real sense of being disconnected. No longer does the caregiver know about everything that happens in a loved-one's day.

This isn't always such a bad thing. Seniors, too, appreciate their privacy.

With the introduction of new federal privacy regulations in 2003, assisted living residences have become more careful about sharing information, even with family members. The facility that you have selected may not be a healthcare facility in the legal sense of the term. But everyone even remotely connected to health care is being strongly encouraged by their legal advisors to follow the same rules that apply to doctors and hospitals.

The big question for families is: what information *will* be passed on, and to whom?

■ Is there any particular paperwork that the facility must have on file to be able to share information with you?

_____

_____

_____

■ Under what circumstances will the facility call a family member?

_____

_____

_____

■ Under what circumstances will the facility call the doctor?

_____

_____

_____

■ Will other professionals who come into the facility (doctors, home care agencies, etc.) honor health care information releases that are on file at the facility, or will family members have to have one for each provider?

_____

_____

_____

■ In the event of a medical emergency, who is reponsible for calling 911? How will the family be notified?

_____

_____

_____

CHAPTER NINE

Who's Who?

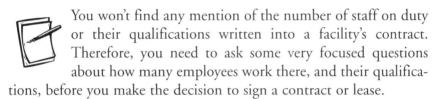 You won't find any mention of the number of staff on duty or their qualifications written into a facility's contract. Therefore, you need to ask some very focused questions about how many employees work there, and their qualifications, before you make the decision to sign a contract or lease.

If the assisted living residence you're considering is licensed by your state, there will be definite state rules and regulations about the number of staff who must be on duty at different times of the day, and the amount and kind of training these staff members must have.

If the home you are considering isn't licensed, then there is no official set of regulations or guidelines that the home has to follow. It will be your duty to probe for accurate information about who works there.

State regulations for licensed facilities will specify the acceptable state "minimums." The best assisted living facilities will exceed their state minimum requirements.

If you're looking at a licensed facility, ask for a copy of the "staffing ratios." This document, sometimes called a "Disclosure Statement," will spell out how many staff members the facility will have on duty during different times of the day. When you visit, compare what you see in this document to the actual number of staff in the building, and their duties.

Remember that administrators, kitchen help, housekeeping and jani-
torial workers aren't providing hands-on care to residents, but they
may be counted among the number of staff "present."

Divide the number of residents in the facility by the number of actual personal care workers. This will give you the ratio of caregiving
employees to residents (the real staffing ratio).

- How many residents does it appear that each personal care
  worker will have to be responsible for during the day?
  At night?

  _____

  _____

  _____

Even the smallest, professionally run facility should have some training requirements for employees.

- What training do new employees receive? CPR? Infection
  Control? Hands-on patient care? Dementia management
  techniques?

  _____

  _____

  _____

- Does everyone working in the facility, from the Administrator to the lowliest garden worker, participate in training?

  _____

  _____

  _____

- Does the facility provide cross-training, so that if necessary the Administrator can give a bath and the chef can help a confused resident?

  _____

  _____

  _____

- Who provides the training? Does a local staff member teach? Do representatives come from the "home office" to provide training? Are educators brought in from the outside to supplement with specialized training?

  _____

  _____

  _____

- How much additional training is provided each year for all employees?

  _____

  _____

  _____

In the small care home, the staff will most likely be either the home-owners themselves, or one or two caregivers who live in the home with the residents. Unless it was provided on a previous job, any training will probably have been brief and informal.

Ask to see copies of any certifications or licenses that you are told the caregivers in a small home have received. Basic first aid and CPR should be the bare minimum. Check that these certificates are still valid. Regular re-testing is required to keep them current.

What Do All These Titles Mean?

The large, multi-apartment assisted living residence will have many, many employees. Among those that you will be most involved with if your loved-one moves in, are:

The Manager

Many states require simply that the manager of a licensed assisted living facility be a high school graduate. What formal education does the manager have in long-term care? Does he or she have a degree or a certificate?

> ■ Is there a requirement that everyone who occupies the position of Manager or Administrator at this facility have completed a specific level of education?
>
> _____
>
> _____
>
> _____

■ What happens if this Administrator leaves? Is there the possibility that a less trained individual might be hired as a replacement?

_____

_____

_____

The Nurse

Everyone feels more comfortable if there is a nurse available, "just in case." Is there a nurse on staff? If so, is the nurse working exclusively at this particular facility, or is she dividing her time among two or more places? If she works a five-day week, how are the two other days covered?

■ Is the nurse a state-licensed, registered nurse? Is he or she an RN (Registered Nurse) or an LVN/LPN? A Licensed Vocational Nurse (LVN) or Licensed Practical Nurse (LPN) has fewer years of training than an RN. Any of these three designations is okay.

_____

_____

_____

If the "nurse" is in fact an aide, or a personal care attendant who has taken a certification course, the facility does not have a "nurse" on staff.

Food Service Manager / Chef

Food is *the* most talked-about, and most complained-about, subject in assisted living residences everywhere. Consistent and good quality food is extremely important. Brochures and advertisements often talk about restaurant-style meals, executive chefs with celebrity backgrounds, and nutritionists on staff.

- Who is really doing the cooking in this particular facility? A famous chef who "consults" may have never stepped into the building. The nutritionist based in the home office may have created six weeks worth of printed menus to be cycled through by the local cooks.

_____

_____

_____

■ ■ ■

The brochure went on and on about the consulting chef who used to cook at the White House. Well, we never saw him. We never saw the platters of shrimp that were on the cover of the brochure, either, except once when they were hosting the Chamber of Commerce in the dining room.

— Melanie

■ ■ ■

- Does the person doing the actual day-to-day cooking have any professional kitchen experience?

_____

_____

_____

- Who cooks on the cook's days or hours off?

_____

_____

_____

- Does the cook have any experience cooking for people with dietary restrictions, or for finicky eaters?

_____

_____

_____

Activity Director

The Activity Director is responsible for organizing and facilitating all the recreational activities that take place, both inside and outside of the facility. This is a staff position that you will find only in facilities with enough residents to make the cost worthwhile. Small residences will have limited, or no, formal activity programs.

You should have already checked out the activity calendar. Not every resident will be interested in being part of large groups that require sitting in a circle. A program limited to chair exercises in the morning and bingo in the afternoon isn't very exciting. The kinds of activities you see on the program should be events that you think your elder might be interested in attending.

Of course, not everyone is a social being. If your elder has never been a person who likes group activities, then a move to assisted living isn't likely to change that. You shouldn't expect it to.

That said, a good Activity Director can make or break the atmosphere of a facility. Active and involved residents are less likely to be unhappy residents.

■ What educational background does the Activity Director have? Does he or she have certification in particular kinds of activities, such as music, drama, exercise, or art? Which ones?

_____

_____

_____

■ If dementia is an issue for your prospective resident, what specialized training does the Activity Director have, if any, in this very specialized area? What outside help is brought in for these activities?

_____

_____

_____

■ ■ ■

When we were first looking for a good Alzheimer's place for my aunt, we visited one that I would never go back to. It was activity time and they had everyone sitting in a circle. There was a radio on that was playing really loud rock music. The little twit leading the group wanted them to do a follow-the-leader clapping game. Some of the residents were getting really upset and trying to leave. She kept pushing them back into their chairs. Then she'd grab their hands and try to make them clap. It was awful. One poor man tried to bite her. I didn't blame him. I wanted to bite her myself.

— Rachel

■ ■ ■

■ If the Activity Director is absent, on leave, or on vacation, who takes over?

_____

_____

_____

■ Does the Activity Director drive the bus or van? What level of driver's license does he or she have, and has the driver been given any special driver education or certification?

_____

_____

_____

Medication Aide

The Medication Aide is often the person who actually "passes meds" or distributes medications to residents. In a small home the "medication aide" will be the same caregiver who attends to most or all of the residents' needs. In a larger facility managing medications may be the primary job function for this particular employee. In either case:

- Who supervises the Medication Aide?

  _____

  _____

  _____

- What certification or training does the Medication Aide have?

  _____

  _____

  _____

- What education does the Medication Aide have about potential side effects or reactions?

  _____

  _____

  _____

- When the appointed Medication Aide is away from the facility, who fills in? What is that person's training?

  _____

  _____

- What precautions are taken to insure that possibly potent drugs are kept secure?

  _____

  _____

  _____

■ What written medication records does the Medication Aide keep?

_____

_____

_____

■ Who is in charge of ordering medications from the pharmacy or calling the physician to request refill authorizations?

_____

_____

■ What steps are taken to insure that medications are ordered in a timely manner so that a resident doesn't run out of medication?

_____

_____

_____

■ Will there be any problems if you want to review the medication records and count the number of doses in stock to confirm that medications have been given properly?

_____

_____

_____

Direct Care Staff

By whatever title, the aides, personal care attendants, resident assistants, etc., these are the people who have the most direct contact with residents on a day-to-day basis. A good direct caregiver, one who respects and honestly cares about the emotional and physical well-being of residents, can make a significant difference in the quality of a resident's life. A poor caregiver, one who has little respect for residents and who treats them roughly, will quickly undo everything good about a facility, no matter how fancy or modern it is.

Sadly, direct caregivers are almost always the poorest paid employees. As a result, there is almost always high turnover among caregivers in a large facility – sometimes topping 100% a year. In small homes, pay is often better, but turnover will happen because of employee burnout. A caregiver who spends 24 or more hours at a time with needy residents can easily become over-tired and short-tempered.

■ What is the caregiver turnover rate in this facility? What is the facility doing to reduce turnover and build employee loyalty?

_____

_____

_____

■ What are the credentials of direct caregivers? How much education, formal and employer-provided, are they required to have?

_____

_____

_____

- What special dementia training have they had, if this is important to you?

  _____

  _____

  _____

Good communication between resident and caregiver is vitally important. For some residents communication will be made more difficult by hearing or speech problems. How fluent in English are the caregivers? If they speak the language, are they comprehensible? Many caregivers have very strong accents. This is not a reflection on the caregiver or the quality of care he or she may deliver. But inability to understand a heavy accent can make residents anxious and may lead to serious mistakes and misunderstandings. Try to talk to some of the caregivers during your tour of the facilities.

- How does the facility assess the communication abilities of caregivers before they are hired?

  _____

  _____

  _____

- If many caregivers are not native English speakers, are they in the habit of speaking to each other in their native language while they are working with residents?

  _____

  _____

Many older folks ultimately decide to move to assisted living because they're concerned about being alone at night – or their families are concerned. Nighttime is also the time when there are the fewest staff members on duty in any residence.

In a small home with only one caregiver present, the caregiver may be sleeping. Some small homes use baby monitors or a similar device so that the caregiver can hear signs of distress.

- In a small home, how is the caregiver made aware of problems during the night?

    _____

    _____

    _____

In a larger residence, the presence and number of staff that are awake at night will depend on both the licensing regulations covering the facility and the characteristics of its residents.

- How many staff members are awake and on duty at night?

    _____

    _____

- Where are they generally stationed, and how do residents call for them if necessary?

    _____

    _____

    _____

■ If one staff member is responsible for monitoring more than one wing or floor, how does the facility insure that call bells will be heard and answered?

_____

_____

_____

CHAPTER TEN

The Dining Room

 Unlikely as it might sound, in a large assisted living facility, even when the food is good, the dining room is often the public room with the most questions and problems. Here are some of the most common:

Assigned Tables

Everybody does it. Large facilities like to assign residents to tables in the dining room because it makes taking a head count at every meal easier. If a resident isn't at a meal, the empty place is immediately obvious.

Unless they're really lucky in their seat assignments, residents tend to dislike assigned tables. Mealtime is a social time, and everyone prefers to socialize with people of their own choosing.

In facilities where seating is assigned, the newest resident often gets "stuck" with the tablemate that no one else wants to eat with. As places open up at other tables, residents who were seated with the "outcast" will ask to be moved to those vacant seats. So, the newest resident is often the odd man out who is forced to sit with the unpleasant resident until a "better" place opens up.

■ ■ ■

When my mother moved in, they put her at a table with two other people – one with serious Alzheimer's and one who is stone deaf. Mom has some health problems, but her mind is sharp. After about four months she got up the nerve to ask for a different table. Now the most recent arrival is sitting at Mom's old place. It doesn't look like anyone can stand to sit there long.

— Gerald

■ ■ ■

A common reply to the question of whether residents have seating options is, "People like routines, and our residents tend to sit at the same place all the time."

That may be true, but it begs the question. Do residents *have* to sit at the same place for every meal, or do they have a choice of sitting wherever, and with whomever, they choose?

> ■ Do residents have a choice of where they will sit in the dining room? Can they eat breakfast at one table, and dinner at another, depending on whom they feel like sitting with?
>
> _____
>
> _____
>
> _____

Mobility Equipment

Strangely enough, some assisted living residences don't welcome wheelchairs or walkers in the dining room. Residents living in these facilities have to be able to "park" their mobility devices and walk to the table, or a staff member will remove the wheelchair or walker when the resident is seated and park it outside the dining room.

Check this out on your tour. When you see chairs and walkers parked outside the dining room, ask questions. If you don't see someone eating in a wheelchair, wonder why. It is an unusual assisted living residence that doesn't have several residents who use equipment to get around. If the resident has to ask for help to leave the table, then the emphasis is on her disability, rather than on her ability to be independent.

The table settings are also revealing. The easier it is to clean a table after meals, the more institutional the feel. Granted, many people in assisted living can be messy eaters. Bare tables and paper napkins are easy to clean up. But it is interesting to observe that, the nicer the dining room looks, the more the residents will try to observe the customs of finer dining. If the table settings look like something from an elementary school or a hospital, then the residents' table manners will often decline to match.

> ■ Are tables in the dining room of large residences set with a "cloth" tablecloth, a plastic cover, or none at all?
>
> _____ _____
>
> _____
>
> _____

If you're looking at a small care home, then residents will most often eat in a family setting at the kitchen table. Finer table settings aren't appropriate in the family kitchen.

Hours

Moving from home to a group living situation means the loss of a lot of freedom. One of the losses that residents feel the most is the ability to eat whenever they choose. The greater the flexibility of mealtime hours, the better.

■ What are the hours that breakfast, the noon meal, and the evening meal are served?

_____

_____

_____

■ Is everyone expected to be in the dining room at a particular time on the dot, or is there a time span when people can choose to eat (i.e., from 11:30 to 1:00 for the noon meal)?

_____

_____

_____

CHAPTER ELEVEN

The Food

For the resident, food is one of the most important criteria in evaluating an assisted living facility. If the food, the dining room, and the meal service are very good, then the residents will let a lot of other little problems slide. If the food and the dining experience leave something to be desired then the complaints about anything and everything else will multiply like locusts.

Keep in mind that one of the first places a facility will attempt to cut corners is in the food. As this is being written, the average daily food budget in larger assisted living residences is less than $4 per day per resident, according to the author's own survey of assisted living administrators.

Some facilities say that their residents aren't interested in getting up and coming to a hot breakfast at a particular time. So they just set out a "continental" breakfast of coffee, juices, cold cereal and muffins in the morning.

This is great for the resident who has never been – and never will be – a breakfast eater. However, the gentleman who wants and looks forward to his pancakes and sausage every morning probably won't be too happy.

■ If the resident isn't an early riser, are there options for a later morning meal?

_____

_____

Menus

Just as group living residents must give up a certain amount of freedom in choosing *when* they'll eat, they also lose the opportunity to choose *what* they'll eat. Imagine knowing that, for the rest of your life, you will have to eat whatever is put in front of you.

If a resident has never been able to stomach creamed corn, and it turns up on the menu as regular as clockwork twice a month, there are going to be complaints. Large facility or small home, there should be some choices at every meal.

■ Are menu choices available at every meal, or is everyone served the same thing?

_____

_____

_____

■ Can a sandwich or fruit be substituted for the standard hot meal if it doesn't appeal to a resident?

_____

_____

_____

■ If the largest meal of the day is served at noon, is the evening meal usually a sandwich?

_____

_____

_____

■ If the facility offers menu options, how are selections made by residents and communicated to the kitchen? For instance, does the resident circle items on a printed sheet at every meal? This could be difficult for those with vision problems or dementia. In that case, how does the dining room staff help with the selection?

_____

_____

_____

■ ■ ■

My husband likes to eat. He really likes to eat. Where he is now, they give everyone a little paper menu at each meal so they can circle which entree, which soup, which dessert, and so on. He circled everything on the paper – and they brought him everything. I finally had to call a meeting with the dining room staff and say, "Look, he's lived here for a year. You know he doesn't remember what he asked for, so give him one selection of each – no more!" It worked. I don't have to buy him larger clothes every few months now.

— Lorraine

■ ■ ■

■ Some facilities use a monthly rotating menu with options. Does the resident chooses all his or her meals for a 30 day period, which then repeats until changed?

_____

_____

_____

Not too many people know what they'll want to eat in three weeks. If the resident doesn't care for a particular meal choice, making changes to one of 30 days on a printout is cumbersome.

Snacks

We are programmed in the United States to eat three meals a day. Children are often discouraged from having between-meal snacks because, "It will ruin your appetite for dinner."

As we get older, we're inclined to eat less at meals. A small snack in the middle of the afternoon or later in the evening often makes up for eating fewer calories at meals. Nutritionists have actually encouraged this kind of "grazing" as fundamentally a much healthier way of eating.

■ Are snacks easily available during the day?

_____

_____

_____

- What do the snacks consist of?

_____

_____

_____

Not eating enough, or forgetting to eat, are problems that can crop up later even if they weren't a problem at move-in. When an older person isn't eating adequately, it is very important that nutritious between-meal snacks be part of the care plan.

- If a resident would benefit from the extra calories of a snack, but isn't inclined to nibble without reminders, will someone directly offer the snack? Remember, there may be an extra charge for "reminders."

_____

_____

_____

- If a resident is supposed to have a specialty snack, like a supplemental calorie drink, will the family have to provide this item? If so, will it be stored in a place where other residents don't have access?

_____

_____

_____

■ Will an "order," or a prescription from the doctor, be required in order for the facility to regularly offer a supplemental calorie drink (Ensure, Boost, etc.)?

_____

_____

_____

Special Diets

Diabetes, high blood pressure, kidney diseases, allergies...the list of medical conditions that might call for dietary adjustments or restrictions is almost endless. It is a rare person who reaches the age of 80 without being instructed by the doctor to "watch" or "avoid" certain foods.

Religious beliefs and lifestyle choices may also be reasons for dietary restrictions.

Most facilities don't offer special diet menus. It would be difficult to cook all of the possible combinations for every possible diet. In addition, many facilities don't want the medical liability that comes with offering special dietary meals.

Most assisted living facilities suggest that residents should be able to maintain their individual diets without a problem by choosing from among the foods they offer routinely. This may or may not work for your particular elder.

■ Does the facility offer special-diet menus, or are residents expected to select the most appropriate food from the menu for themselves?

_____

_____

_____

■ Can the facility accommodate residents with religious or philosophical dietary restrictions? Are kosher or vegetarian meals available?

_____

_____

_____

A resident's need to stick with a diet, such as a low sugar diet for the diabetic, or a low-salt diet for high blood pressure, often conflicts with what a resident would really like to eat. This conflict is difficult for an assisted living facility to manage because they have to honor the resident's right to make independent decisions.

Unless a resident is incompetent, the facility usually won't be able to force compliance with dietary restrictions.

■ How does the facility handle the situation when a diabetic wants two desserts? Are salt shakers available on all the tables all the time, or does a resident have to ask for salt (so that staff can monitor and discourage, if necessary)?

_____

_____

_____

Special Circumstances

There will always be things that are unique to an individual. How a facility attempts to adjust to these differences will spell the difference between an excellent and a so-so, or poor, residence.

■ If a resident is forgetful or has difficulty reading a clock, will the staff remind the resident about meals?

_____

_____

_____

■ If necessary, will someone walk the resident to the dining room?

_____

_____

_____

■ What are the extra charges for these services, if they aren't already covered at the care level you are paying for?

_____

_____

_____

■ Can meals be served on a tray in the resident's room? What are the requirements for this to be approved? Is there an extra charge for this service?

_____

_____

_____

■ If a resident wants to have a guest, how far in advance does the kitchen have to be notified?

_____

_____

_____

■ Can guests have a private meal in the resident's room, or is there a private dining room?

_____

_____

_____

CHAPTER TWELVE

Medication

 Inability to keep track of medications, or to take them properly, is one of the primary reasons for an elder to move into assisted living.

The contract will probably commit the facility to medication "supervision" or "assistance." It is a good idea to go a little deeper and get some specific questions answered.

Distribution of Medications

More than half of the residents in any particular assisted living facility, whatever the size, will need help with managing their medications. How the facility actually performs this is critically important.

In the small assisted living home, medications will most probably be passed out just the same way they would be at your home. The caregiver(s) will be in charge. The medications are most often stored in a kitchen cabinet.

In a bigger facility there will be a central area where medications are stored and prepared for distribution to residents. The method of distribution will vary.

It should be the resident's right to keep and manage both prescription and over-the-counter medications, as long as the resident is capable of doing so. Some facilities resist this idea and require that all medications be turned over to the staff. This can be demeaning to the capable resident. It can also have negative consequences: residents may not be comfortable requesting PRN, or "as needed" medications, such as antacids, intestinal gas relievers, or pain relievers. Some will go without rather than have to announce their need to a staff member.

■ If the resident is competent and able to manage them, will he or she be permitted to keep medications in the room or apartment and take them without supervision?

_____

_____

_____

There isn't a perfect way to distribute medications to a large number of people on a regular basis. There are two primary methods used in large residential facilities: a "medication cart" is moved from room to room, or residents come to a central place to receive their medications at specified times of the day. Because there are pros and cons to both methods, you should know how the facility handles medications so you can work with them when the inevitable problem crops up.

If medication is distributed to the resident in his room, and the resident happens to be in another part of the facility at that moment, the Medication Aide will have to track the resident down.

If the resident has to remember to come to a central dispensing station for medication there is a good chance that doses will be missed. Or, the Medication Aide will then have to track down the resident who forgets, possibly at an additional service charge.

Medication passed out in the dining room can be lost in a plate of food, spilled on the floor, hidden under the plate, taken by the wrong person, or otherwise misused. Residents should always be handed their medication and they should be observed until they have properly taken it. Medication should *never, ever* be simply placed in a cup at the resident's plate.

- Are medications brought to the resident in the resident's room?

  _____

  _____

  _____

- Are medications placed by the resident's plate in the dining room?

  _____

  _____

  _____

- Does the resident have to remember to come to a central station to get medication?

  _____

  _____

  _____

Preferred Pharmacy

Many facilities are now preferring prepackaged medications, where all of an individual's medications are packaged together for a particular dose time. All of the breakfast medications are packaged together, all of the noon medications are together, and so on.

This system is a great convenience for the facility, and it does seem to reduce some medication errors. However, in some cases it can more than double the cost of a resident's medications. Be particularly wary of "preferred pharmacy" issues if the resident uses a Medicare HMO or other insurance that requires you to use designated pharmacies.

- Does the facility require that medications be supplied by an in-house or contracted pharmacy?

  _____

  _____

  _____

- If the family would rather buy medications from another pharmacy and bring them in, will there be a "penalty" charge because they aren't prepackaged, and distributing them requires more work on the part of the staff?

  _____

  _____

  _____

■　■　■

My father's prescriptions are covered by his insurance company and he gets them from a mail-order pharmacy. We were ordering them and taking them up there, and it was working fine. Then they decided they wanted everyone's medicine to come from the same place. Their pharmacy is not covered by his insurance, and it would have cost more than $400 a month more to pay full price. We had to move him to another place. I'm very angry because another move was really hard on him, but he couldn't afford it.

— Randall

■　■　■

- If you think you'd prefer to use the facility's recommended pharmacy, are there any add-ons like delivery charges?

_____

_____

_____

- If you have insurance for medications, is the facility's preferred pharmacy covered?

_____

_____

_____

Quantity Limits

On occasion, when a resident is taking a large number of medications ("polypharmacy"), the facility may want to add on an additional charge because of the extra time needed for tracking and keeping records. This shouldn't be an issue if all the medications are prepackaged by the pharmacy.

- Is there a limit to the number of medications a resident may take without additional charges?

_____

_____

_____

■ Is there a limit to the number of times per day that medication will be dispensed without additional charge?

_____

_____

_____

"Oral" or "Topical" Medications Only

Assisted living facilities are not licensed to provide skilled nursing services. This can turn into a problem if a resident needs to receive a medication by injection.

Diabetics often come up against this restriction. As long as the resident can manage diabetes independently – doing her own "finger sticks" and taking oral medication, the diabetic resident is almost always welcome in an assisted living facility.

Some facilities are happy to assist a resident with the "finger stick" blood sugar check. Others say that, because pricking the finger involves going through the skin, they cannot perform this test.

This seems to be one of those situations that is open to interpretation. If the facility wants to care for diabetic residents, they will usually find that it's possible to do what is necessary as far as finger-sticks go.

Most, but not all, assisted living facilities will say that they aren't able to care for a resident who needs injections.

■ ■ ■

I thought everything else about the place was just perfect for my mother. My wife and I decided that she would go by every morning, and I would go every evening on my way home from work to do her finger stick blood glucose test, because her residence isn't licensed to prick her finger. I admit we didn't think it through very well, and no one there talked with us about it. Pretty soon we realized we couldn't ever have a day off. Would you believe we planned a wedding around it? We did that for almost eight months before we came to our senses. You don't think real clearly when you're so caught up in it.

— Heinz

■　■　■

If the prospective resident is using Insulin, or needs regular injections for any medical condition, get a clear understanding with the facility about what their staff can and cannot do. If injections aren't necessary now, but there is any chance that they might be required in the future, it is important to know what your future options might be.

■ What is the residential policy about injected medications and diabetic blood sugar tests?

_____

_____

_____

■ Will the need to receive medications by injection mean that the resident will have to move because the facility cannot administer the medication?

_____

_____

_____

CHAPTER THIRTEEN

Personal Care

Bathing

If you grew up in the United States, you are probably used to bathing or showering every day. When an assisted living facility talks about assistance with bathing and dressing, most families visualize a nice shower every morning or every evening, just like at home.

Probably not. More likely, the standard routine is a shower two to three times a week. Additional assistance with bathing will almost always be possible for an extra fee.

It's not possible to help everyone shower before breakfast or before bed, so showers will be given throughout the day. The resident could have a shower at ten o'clock in the morning, or in the middle of the afternoon.

The gender of the person helping with the bath is also sometimes an issue. Women residents prefer to be assisted by women. In assisted living, this generally isn't a problem because the majority of workers in the field are women.

On the other hand, if a gentleman would like to have bathing assistance from a male aide, there could be a problem. No facility is likely to be able to promise assistance from a male aide. There simply aren't enough male caregivers available.

■ How many times per week will the resident be helped with a bath?

_____

_____

_____

■ Is there a difference in the fees between "reminder and cueing," "stand-by assistance" and actual hands-on help with bathing?

_____

_____

_____

"Reminder and cueing" means that the caregiver will remind the resident that it is time to bathe, and will coach the resident through the process with words, but without actually having a direct hand in the process.

"Stand-by assistance" means that the aide or caregiver remains very close to the resident, guarding against a fall or other accident. The caregiver may hand the resident the soap, a washcloth or a towel, but the resident washes on his own.

"Hands-on assistance," "direct assistance," or "full care" is for those residents who are physically or mentally in need of being bathed.

Skin Care

Elderly skin tends to be thin and dry, and lotions are sometimes necessary to keep skin from becoming itchy and flaky.

■ Will the care staff help apply lotion routinely?

_____

_____

_____

■ If so, does "routinely" mean only after a bath, or daily?

_____

_____

_____

■ Is skin lotion considered to be a medication requiring an "order" (prescription) from the doctor before an employee can assist with it?

_____

_____

_____

Nail Care

Nail care is something that you really have to ask about specifically. Toenail care is something most facilities won't allow their care staff to do. If toenails aren't cut properly they can become ingrown. Thickened and malformed toenails are common among the elderly. Small nicks can be slow to heal and prone to infection because of diabetes or circulatory problems. The potential for problems is too great

If the resident isn't able to independently maintain his or her feet, most likely a family member will have to assist, or the services of a podiatrist may be necessary.

Some facilities don't think that fingernails pose the same hazards, and some residences include nail care as part of their bathing and grooming services. However, experience indicates that if a facility has a beauty/barber shop on the premises residents are often sent there for manicures. This, of course, is at an additional cost.

"Manicures" are sometimes included as part of the activity schedule, and they are often very popular among the women. Unfortunately, the average elderly man isn't usually thrilled about joining the women for a manicure.

- Is hand and fingernail care included in personal care services?

  _____

  _____

  _____

- Is there an extra charge?

  _____

  _____

  _____

Dressing

"Assistance with dressing" is another one of those phrases that can be wide open to interpretation. You should get an exact definition of what it means in each facility.

It seems that small personal care homes tend to have fairly liberal definitions, and help is usually available whenever necessary. In larger residential facilities, with more residents and a higher resident-to-aide ratio, there may be more formal rules and guidelines.

■ Is assistance with dressing offered seven days a week, or only included on bath days?

_____

_____

_____

■ Is there an extra charge for help with dressing when there is no bath? What is the charge?

_____

_____

_____

■ Does "assistance with dressing" include assisting the resident to wash face and hands, brush teeth and, for men, shave?

_____

_____

_____

It's obvious at many assisted living residences that these services aren't offered on a routine daily basis to residents who need help with hygiene. Often men remain unshaven between bath days. It can sometimes be apparent that teeth and dentures aren't cleaned daily.

■   ■   ■

Even though morning and nighttime denture care was written down on the "care plan", my mother was obviously sleeping with her dentures in. One day I asked the aide about Mother's teeth. The aide said she didn't know Mother wore dentures. They clack a bit when she talks, so I found that hard to believe.

— Alyce

■   ■   ■

■ Does "assistance with dressing" include helping the resident to choose fresh underwear and clean clothing daily? If the resident resists changing clothing, does the facility make sure that he or she is in fresh and clean clothing between bath days?

_____

_____

_____

■ Does "assistance with dressing" include helping the resident to prepare for bed every night? This includes cleaning teeth, washing the face and changing into bedclothes.

_____

_____

_____

■ Is there an extra charge for evening help if help is provided in the morning?

_____

_____

_____

■ If the resident has an occasional (not routine) accident or spill during the day, will there be an additional charge to help the resident change and clean up? If so, how much?

_____

_____

_____

Toileting

Quite a few residents of assisted living need help with using the bathroom. Some may just need a little guidance in getting there. Others will need help getting in and out of a bed or a chair and into the bathroom. Some will need to be reminded to go on a regular basis. Others will need help managing incontinent briefs.

Remember, an assisted living residence isn't a nursing home, and help isn't always immediately available at the push of a button. If your relative is completely unable to use the toilet unassisted, and he or she is likely to be incontinent if not responded to immediately, you will have to supply incontinent briefs to help with the problem.

Many assisted living facilities are willing to accommodate a resident with "manageable" incontinence. Usually, this means that the resident has a problem with urine only, and the resident is cooperative with wearing briefs, if necessary. If bowel movements present a problem, many assisted living facilities will not accept, or keep, the resident. Be sure you know what the policies are.

- At the level of care you are discussing, how many times per day is incontinent care included?

_____

_____

- What kind of incontinent care is available? "Bowel and bladder," or "bladder" only?

_____

_____

- What is the extra incremental cost if a resident needs more help than the standard schedule allows?

_____

_____

_____

- Does "occasional extra need" mean that the care plan will be increased to the next "level?" Define "occasional."

_____

_____

_____

- If the resident-to-be needs hygiene reminders after using the toilet, how does the facility monitor bathroom use?

_____

_____

_____

Note: if a resident needs frequent or constant hygiene reminders, but the resident is using the toilet on his or her own, it isn't realistic to expect that the staff will know when help was needed. You may be faced with the need to revise the care plan to include a full bath daily. This will increase your costs.

Transferring

"Transferring" is the act of getting up and moving from a bed to a chair, from a chair to a bed, or from anywhere to a standing position. Residents with unstable balance, severe arthritis, or diseases that affect balance, such as stroke or Parkinson's Disease, often need help with transferring.

First and foremost, is the facility you are considering legally permitted to accept residents who can't evacuate the building without assistance in an emergency? Although most residences are, some are not.

If the residence that you are considering is not, then are you prepared to relocate your elder if she becomes unable to transfer on her own?

If a resident needs help with transfers, ask about the facility's policy on the amount of help a resident might need? Many facilities specify that the resident has to be able to transfer with the assistance of just one person. If more than one person is needed to help the resident, then the level of need is too high for the facility to accept.

Many facilities also require that the resident must be able to "bear weight" on at least one foot and be able to pivot the body. What this does is allow the aide to help with stability and prevent falling, while the resident actually carries his own weight. The aide doesn't have to actually lift the resident.

■ If help with transferring is included in the care plan, what will the additional cost be?

_____

_____

_____

■ How many times per day is transfer assistance included, and what will the additional charge(s) be if help is needed more frequently?

_____

_____

_____

Supplies

Families are often surprised to learn that assisted living residents must provide their own personal and hygiene supplies. Standard supplies that must be provided can include bath and hand soap, shampoo and other hair products, lotions, deodorant, razor and shaving creams, facial and toilet tissue. Often the resident is asked to bring a personal shower curtain, tub mat and shower stool.

■ What personal products and supplies will the resident be required to provide?

_____

_____

_____

■ What products and supplies will the facility routinely supply?

_____

_____

_____

■ What products, especially items like incontinent supplies, will the facility order for the resident and bill the resident as they are used?

_____

_____

_____

CHAPTER FOURTEEN

Housekeeping & Laundry

One of the really appealing benefits of moving to an assisted living residence is no longer having to be responsible for housekeeping. Major housekeeping, from bathroom scrubbing thorough vacuuming, should be offered at least once a week. Someone should visit the room daily to empty wastebaskets, make the bed, and generally check for housekeeping needs.

- Within the resident's private space (the room or apartment) how often is routine housekeeping provided?

_____

_____

_____

■ What does housekeeping consist of? Will the cleaning staff vacuum the carpets? Dust all surfaces? Scrub the bathroom, including the floor, commode, shower walls, sink and mirrors? Empty all the wastebaskets?

_____

_____

_____

■ Will housekeeping check the room on a daily basis, empty the wastebaskets and make the bed as part of the base rate?

_____

_____

_____

■ Accidents happen. If the carpet needs to be scrubbed, will there be an extra charge? How much?

_____

_____

_____

■ How often are carpets in residents' rooms cleaned on a routine basis?

_____

_____

_____

If the resident is sensitive to carpet cleaning materials, or any other cleaning and laundry products for that matter, the time to discuss this is before a contract is signed.

Laundry

"Flat" laundry is usually included in the base rate of an assisted living residence. Flat laundry means sheets and towels, and perhaps a bath-mat. No clothing is included in flat laundry.

Flat laundry will usually be collected and washed on a weekly basis. The bed should be remade with clean linen, and clean towels should be placed in the bath. It will usually be the resident's responsibility to have at least two sets of everything, so that there is always something clean and available to use. Some facilities will provide sheets and towels. You have to ask and verify the cost.

■ Does the facility provide any linens, i.e., sheets and towels. If so, what size bed can they accommodate?

_____

_____

_____

Personal laundry usually isn't included in the base rate. If they are able, some residents choose to do their own laundry in machines provided by the facility. Or, many families will take laundry home, where they have more control of how laundry is done.

■ If the facility is going to do personal laundry, what will the additional charge be?

_____

_____

_____

■ Will personal laundry always be done on a particular day of the week?

_____

_____

■ If the resident is forgetful or confused, will someone help gather up the soiled personal laundry so that it is all washed?

_____

_____

_____

■ Will someone assist the resident with putting clean clothing away in the proper place, if necessary?

_____

_____

_____

■ Are there extra charges for this more personal laundry assistance, or is it included?

_____

_____

If the resident is sensitive to laundry detergent, it would be wise for you to plan on taking care of personal laundry for the resident. It is difficult to be certain that special products will be used consistently, even if you supply them.

Resident clothing should also be washable in hot water if the facility is going to be managing laundry. In order to reduce the chance of an infection getting loose in a facility, assisted living residences will be careful to wash clothing and flat laundry thoroughly. They will probably use a hot dryer, too.

If the resident is in the habit of wearing garments that need to be hand washed, or that need other special care, you should not plan on having personal laundry done by the assisted living facility.

CHAPTER FIFTEEN

Safety

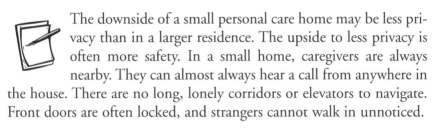 The downside of a small personal care home may be less privacy than in a larger residence. The upside to less privacy is often more safety. In a small home, caregivers are always nearby. They can almost always hear a call from anywhere in the house. There are no long, lonely corridors or elevators to navigate. Front doors are often locked, and strangers cannot walk in unnoticed.

Most of this chapter is devoted to questions that you should ask of large, multi-apartment assisted living residences.

■ Given his or her possible health issues and potential for falls, will your elder be safe in the apartment when the door is closed and no one can see in?

_____

_____

_____

■ Does the facility check on the well-being of residents in their rooms regularly? How, and how often?

_____

_____

_____

■ Does the resident staff make night checks?

_____

_____

_____

If your elder is relatively self-sufficient and reliable, then nightly two-hour checks will be most unwelcome and intrusive. On the other hand, if your elder is confused or in need of close supervision, then routine checks several times a night will be a welcome security.

■ If security checks aren't offered as part of a base service package, what is the extra charge for this service? Can it be added as an individual service without increasing the assessed level of care?

_____

_____

_____

- How will the facility know if a resident is "missing?" Are residents required to sign out when they leave?

  _____

  _____

  _____

- If a resident does appear to be missing, what is the facility's standard procedure? How soon will the authorities be notified? Who, exactly, is notified?

  _____

  _____

  _____

Pull cords are a "safety feature" that many assisted living residences have installed in their rooms and apartments. When the cord is pulled, an alarm will ring, alerting staff to a possible fall or other emergency. Most apartments have a pull cord installed near the toilet and another near the bed. There is usually no extra charge for the availability of a pull cord.

The disadvantage of a pull cord installed on the wall is inaccessibility. If a resident needs help while sitting on the toilet, the pull cord is within reach. It isn't necessarily within reach from the shower.

If a resident needs help while in bed, he may be able to reach the pull cord (if it isn't out of reach behind the headboard). But if he falls anywhere else in the room, he probably won't be able to reach the cord. If he falls in the hallway at night, when no one is around, he certainly won't be able to reach a pull cord. Pull cords aren't especially reassuring.

More reassuring, at a cost, are personal response alarms. A resident wears a personal alarm around the neck or on the wrist. In the event help is needed, the resident pushes a button on the alarm – which can even be worn in the shower – and the designated response person is immediately contacted by phone or beeper.

■ Is a wearable personal emergency alarm offered to residents?

_____

_____

_____

■ Is there an extra fee for a personal alarm?

_____

_____

_____

■ If the facility doesn't offer personal alarms, can the resident buy or lease a unit and designate the facility as the emergency contact?

_____

_____

_____

■ Personal alarms can be bumped or otherwise set off by accident. Does the facility have a policy about false alarms? Will there be a charge for false alarms? How many are allowed?

_____

_____

_____

People come and go throughout the day in a large facility, and it can be difficult to keep track of who is in the building.

- What measures does the facility take to keep potential problem visitors out of the building?

  _____

  _____

  _____

- What time are the doors locked at night, and when are they unlocked in the morning?

  _____

  _____

  _____

- Is there an alarm that will ring if someone opens a door from the inside after hours?

  _____

  _____

  _____

- If the outer door is locked, how do residents and families gain entrance after hours?

  _____

  _____

  _____

■ If residents or families have to wait for a staff member to open the door after hours, the aide may be busy with another resident. Is there a warm, safe place to wait?

_____

_____

_____

■ If a staff member must unlock the door after hours, can the bell be heard when that staff member is in another resident's room?

_____

_____

_____

After safety of "the person" comes safety of "stuff." Every resident has possessions that are personal, valuable to that person, and private.

■ Can residents lock their doors?

_____

_____

■ Who has keys to resident rooms or apartments?

_____

_____

_____

■ Is there a secure place where residents can deposit a reasonable amount of cash for safe keeping?

_____

_____

_____

Every licensed or regulated assisted living residence must provide the fire department with an evacuation plan in case of fire or other emergency. Evacuation routes in the building should be posted. Fire drills are supposed to be held regularly.

■ When was the last fire drill? Naturally, nights aren't a popular time for fire drills. Has the night staff ever participated in one?

_____

_____

_____

■ If there is a loss of electricity, does the night staff have an accessible list of residents who are using oxygen or other critical electrical equipment and who may need immediate assistance in the dark?

_____

_____

_____

California has earthquakes, the mid-west has tornados, Florida and the Gulf have hurricanes, and a lot of places have ice storms and other winter emergencies. In the event of a real emergency, what is the plan for evacuation?

- Does the facility have an evacuation plan?

  _____

  _____

  _____

- Where will residents be taken in the event evacuation is necessary?

  _____

  _____

  _____

- How will residents be transported in an emergency?

  _____

  _____

  _____

CHAPTER SIXTEEN

Transportation

 Just because someone lives in an assisted living residence doesn't mean that he or she can't drive. But chances are good that sooner or later inability to drive will become a problem.

- If the resident is still driving, is there a secure, reserved place to park the car?

  _____

  _____

- Is the parking area well-lit and safe at night?

  _____

  _____

- Is there an additional charge for a parking space?

  _____

  _____

  _____

No longer being able to drive is one of the biggest losses of independence. Access to reliable transportation is very important. Smaller homes will offer limited activities, and transportation will be restricted or not available at all. For the most part, families will be expected to drive their family members wherever they want or need to go.

In larger assisted living residences some amount of transportation is almost always offered. On brochures and lists of services, transportation is often listed as part of the "amenities" offered. On a simple list, though, "transportation" can mean just about anything. It is best to clarify.

- Does the facility provide transportation?

  _____

  _____

- Is there an additional charge for transportation?

  _____

  _____

- Are charges calculated according to distance?

  _____

  _____

  _____

- Is transportation available every day, or only on certain days or hours?

  _____

  _____

  _____

■ Is regular group transportation scheduled to popular department stores (Target, K-Mart, Wal-Mart) drug stores, shopping malls, and the like? How often?

_____

_____

_____

■ Is individual transportation available for trips to places other than the doctor?

_____

_____

_____

■ Must medical appointments be scheduled on specific days of the week if transportation is needed?

_____

_____

_____

■ Is there a maximum number of miles that the facility will drive? Many facilities have a ten-mile limit on the distance they will travel.

_____

_____

_____

■ What kind of vehicle do they use? If the vehicle is a van, is it one that the resident will be able to climb into without difficulty?

_____

_____

_____

■ If the resident uses a wheelchair, is there a lift on the van for the chair? If there is no lift, residents who are confined to wheelchairs will not be able to use the van safely.

_____

_____

_____

■ What insurance does the facility carry for the driver, the van, and the passengers?

_____

_____

_____

■ Is an employee's personal car ever used to transport residents? If so, are the car, the driver and the passenger(s) adequately covered with the appropriate insurance?

_____

_____

_____

CHAPTER SEVENTEEN

Outside Services

The more services a facility can offer to residents on-site, the more attractive the facility will be for both residents and their families. There will be less need to worry about making appointments. Family members won't have to take time off from work quite so often. It is a win/win situation for everyone.

It is not reasonable, or economical, for a facility to try to provide every possible service a resident might need or want. Therefore, many large facilities will "contract" or make arrangements with other service providers, allowing them to either use a permanent dedicated space or come into the facility. The service provider provides the service and keeps the residents' accounts, and then invoices each resident individually.

Some of the outside services most commonly offered in larger assisted living facilities include:

Barber / Beauty Shop

The facility will often provide a room(s) dedicated to hair, and a beautician will maintain a regular schedule there. In very large residences the shop may be staffed every day. In smaller facilities, the beautician may be there one or more days a week. The beautician will usually be available for haircuts and nail care for both men and women, and permanents and other services for the women. The costs are usually in line with the average for shops in the area. Shop owners handle the fees and many residents will have an "account" which is regularly settled by the person who manages the resident's finances.

■   ■   ■

My grandmother's whole life revolved around getting her hair done every week. She never missed. It was the greatest thing when she found out her regular hairdresser could come and do her hair in the beauty shop on a day when it wasn't being used. We're paying the lady who's been cutting her hair for 20 years to come do it just the same way she's always done. It's the best investment we've ever made.

— Grace

■   ■   ■

Physician

Getting out for routine doctor visits can be especially taxing. It isn't easy to make doctor appointments if the patient is restricted by transportation limits or mobility issues.

Some assisted living facilities are making house-call arrangements with one or more physicians. The physician, or in some instances a nurse practitioner or a physician's assistant, will visit the facility on a regular basis. Patients will be seen either in their own apartments or in a "clinic" room maintained by the facility.

Without having to leave home, the resident has the opportunity to have regular health checks, necessary laboratory tests, and medications prescribed or prescriptions renewed.

If the facility that you are considering does have a physician making "visits" to residents, this can be a godsend to both residents and their families. Because the residents are almost all elderly, there should be no question that the doctor will accept Medicare.

Medical Home Health Care

When a resident needs regular treatment for a condition requiring a nurse, a physical or occupational therapist, or a speech therapist – and if getting out for treatment is difficult or impossible – home visits can be ordered by a doctor. With this kind of homecare the resident does not have to go out to a clinic or other facility for care. If it meets their guidelines Medicare covers the treatment.

Many facilities have informal arrangements with one or more Medicare homecare agencies to provide this kind of care to their residents. The nurses and therapists know their way around the building, and the staff knows the professionals who are regularly coming in.

If you would prefer to use the services of another Medicare agency that isn't part of this informal arrangement, it is always your right to do so.

Podiatrist

In the same vein, many older people need assistance with foot care. Because the nails on older feet are often difficult to maintain, many assisted living facilities are reluctant, or are actually not allowed, to handle toenail care. So, a podiatrist who makes house-calls is invaluable.

■   ■   ■

My husband is diabetic, and he had a stroke a few years ago. He drags his foot, and every now and then he gets a sore spot that won't heal. Since last year the podiatrist has been working with the home health nurse, and together they cleared up three different places. Without them, I think he would have lost his foot by now. They are a wonderful team.

— Sheila

■   ■   ■

Podiatrists who make house-calls to assisted living residences will most likely also be more than willing to bill Medicare for any covered treatments. Be aware, however, that Medicare does not cover all podiatric care. If you're interested in this service, and if it's available, check with the podiatrist about what will, and what will not, be covered.

Dentist

Much more rare is the dentist who will make visits to an assisted living facility. But, very occasionally, this kind of treatment is available on site. If so, be aware that Medicare almost never covers dental services, and you will have to make private arrangements to pay the dentist.

Optometrist

Optometrists don't usually visit assisted living facilities, either. But they do often visit patients in nursing homes, and if the facility is part of a larger complex with a nursing home, the optometrist may also see assisted living residents. Like the dentist, Medicare does not cover the services of an optometrist.

Psychological Services

Like optometrists, mental health professionals do not often visit assisted living residences because the reimbursement they receive from Medicare is so low, and the travel time involved is too costly. When they do, they can be a great addition to the care team. Psychological services *may* be covered by Medicare, but it will be at a lower reimbursement rate than for medical care. The facility will be able to tell you whether they have access to a good psychologist who will see residents "at home."

Book-Mobile

If the city or town has a mobile library, it may make regular visits to the facility. Although it can't possibly have the selection of the regular library, the book-mobile is a wonderful service to residents who love to read but can't easily travel to the library. Also, some facilities have a small on site library made up primarily of donations.

■ What outside service providers regularly come into the residence?

_____

_____

_____

CHAPTER EIGHTEEN

Absences

■ ■ ■

They were so nice about it. When my wife broke her hip, she was in the hospital and rehab for almost two months. I didn't even have to ask...right away they took all of her meals and personal care off the bill. They kept her plants watered, and they even took care of her bird while she was gone. When she came home, her room was like she'd never left. I would recommend (this place) to everyone.

— Wallace

■ ■ ■

Like anyone else, someone living in assisted living will probably be away overnight from time to time. There are visits to family members' homes for vacations or holidays. There may be hospital stays. What is the policy on absences from the facility?

- Will there be any reduction of fees if a resident is away from the facility?

_____

_____

_____

- Is there a minimum period before a fee reduction is made (i.e. after a three-day absence, but not for one night)?

_____

_____

_____

- What fees are reduced?

_____

_____

_____

- Since fees and rent are usually paid in advance, how are any refunds handled?

_____

_____

_____

CHAPTER NINETEEN

Hospice

■ ■ ■

Mama passed away last year in her own room. She went peacefully in her sleep the way she wanted to – with no tubes, no needles, and all of us with her. If she hadn't been able to stay there, she would have had to go to a nursing home or a hospital, and she would have hated that. The hospice people were wonderful. Whenever we needed them, they were there. Toward the end, the nurse even stayed all night. The day after Mama died the hospice chaplain came back and visited with all of her friends who lived there. He helped us put together a memorial service for the residents. Everyone came, even a lot of the aides who were supposed to be off duty that day.

— Louise

■ ■ ■

Just about every rule can be broken. The rule about being able to stay on in an assisted living residence when care needs increase substantially is no exception. Hospice is the service that can make this possible.

Hospice care provides home-based medical and emotional support for the terminally ill patient. The intent is to keep the patient pain-free and comfortable, rather than aggressively treat an illness.

Most people want to live out their remaining time on earth at home, rather than in a hospital or nursing home. People who live in assisted living are no exception. For someone who has lived there for a length of time, the residence has become home.

If a resident has a terminal illness that is expected (not required) to result in death within six months, and if "cure" is no longer a possibility, then hospice care at home in the residence is a viable option for some families.

Medicare covers hospice care, with the possible exception of small co-payments for some medications and equipment. A team of physicians, nurses, aides and social workers collaborates closely with both the family and the residence to provide care to the individual and support for the family and caregivers.

Keep this in mind: if you're thinking about Hospice the need for someone to be with the patient in the room or apartment will steadily increase. Although Hospice sends nurses and aides as necessary to provide care, they can't usually stay with the patient for extended periods of time.

The facility does not have the capacity to provide a staff person to stay with a resident for hours at a time, either.

So, if you're considering Hospice care in an assisted living residence, and you can't stay with your loved one, you will eventually have to hire an aide. A sitter may be adequate in the beginning, but an aide will be necessary if the patient becomes bed-bound or needs care from someone with training.

If the cost of providing Hospice care in an assisted living residence becomes prohibitive, Hospice care can be provided in a nursing home setting, as well.

Because it isn't possible to predict ahead of time when or whether a terminal illness may occur, it would be a good idea to get some basic information from the facility before you make a move-in commitment:

■ Does the facility permit residents to receive Hospice care, even if it means the resident may become confined to bed?

_____

_____

_____

■ Has the residence worked with any particular agency providing Hospice care?

_____

_____

_____

People who are receiving Hospice care are expected to pass away at home. Generally, when a patient enrolls in a Hospice program, he or she agrees that CPR or other resuscitation measures will not be done. Also, where permitted by law, being enrolled in a Hospice program also means that paramedics (911) will not be called in the event of the patient's death. Instead, the Hospice nurse will be called, and he or she will take care of all the necessary details.

■ What is the residence policy regarding "Do-Not-Resuscitate" orders or calling 911 for residents who are receiving Hospice care?

_____

_____

_____

CHAPTER TWENTY

Negotiated Risk

As much as most of us would like to keep all the people we love completely safe from harm, it simply isn't possible. Life is never completely free of risk.

Sometimes, when a resident is in the habit of doing things that might result in illness or injury, an assisted living facility will indicate that they are willing to discuss a separate and specific "negotiated risk" contract.

Negotiating risk means being willing to accept the possibility of accident or injury to the resident in exchange for allowing the resident freedom. For example, everyone may agree that the elder will be permitted to continue using a walker, and therefore will probably take an occasional fall, rather than being required to use a wheelchair.

■   ■   ■

My grandfather has always been a real couch potato. He was always sitting in his recliner, except when he was in the dining room. After a while he got so weak that he needed a walker, and he started falling in the corridor on the way down there.

The manager finally made a deal with him: Either he would have to come to exercise class every day or he would have to move to a nursing home. He didn't like it one bit, but he did it. He still has to use the walker, but he's not falling as much.

And he actually made a friend in the class, the first one he's made there. They spend time together almost every day griping and complaining about everything, and having a real fine time.

— Steven

■　　■　　■

Or, a resident with manageable Alzheimer's may be permitted to stay in an unsecured facility that has become familiar, even though there is a chance that he might start wandering and get lost as the disease progresses. In this case, a non-removable identification bracelet should be required as part of the contract.

The negotiated risk contract might be offered as a means of allowing a resident to stay, when otherwise she would be asked to move out.

Be aware that this specialized contract or agreement, if it is offered, is intended to protect the facility – not the resident – from liability should an injury or accident happen.

On the other hand, be aware that no one can prevent every accident. Most of us would rather take a little risk than have even more independence taken away.

- Has the facility ever offered to compromise with a resident about something that could possibly be dangerous for the resident (not someone else)? What kinds of things have they been willing to negotiate about with residents and their families?

_____

_____

_____

CHAPTER TWENTY-ONE

Moving In

 Most people prefer to move on the weekend, when friends and family are available to help with the organizing and heavy lifting. Most assisted living facilities prefer that new residents move in on a weekday.

Check this out early in your decision-making process. So often, families sign the contract and schedule movers before they realize that the weekend day they have chosen for the move is not going to be satisfactory to the assisted living residence.

Most often their argument is that not all of the facility's personnel will be available on the weekend. The administrator, or the nurse, or another necessary individual usually does not work on the weekends, and has to be present when the new resident comes in. The orientation or the assessment will be delayed, and the new resident will be deprived of the professional support that would have been available Monday through Friday during business hours.

This raises the question about an apparent lack of personnel and services on weekends. Do use the opportunity to address any lingering questions you might have about weekend life in this particular facility. If they are so understaffed that they don't want new residents coming in on the weekend, what activities and support are available to everyone else on the weekend?

Address this issue up front, and you will likely be able to agree on a weekend move.

■ Are new residents permitted to move in on the weekend?

_____

_____

_____

■ Are staff allowed to assist with any part of the move?
For instance, can a maintenance worker help carry a heavy
mattress?

_____

_____

_____

■ Is there any equipment, such as a dolly or wheeled cart,
available to help with moving heavy items?

_____

_____

_____

CHAPTER TWENTY-TWO

Moving Out

The average length of stay in an assisted living residence is between 18 months and two years. Just as every resident of an assisted living facility had a unique reason for moving in, everyone has a unique reason for moving out. Sometimes it is voluntary – the resident is well enough to go back home, or is moving in with family. Sometimes it is due to a change for the worse, which requires a higher level of care.

Your contract should clearly spell out how relocation will be handled. Read the contract very carefully, so you understand everything.

■ ■ ■

When he got too sick to live alone I found a lovely small care home where my father could have hospice care "at home," rather than in a nursing home. Just 23 days later, much sooner than we all expected, he passed away in his new "home."

I was under a lot of pressure to find a place for him, and I admit I did read the contract, but I didn't really understand what I signed. Turns out the contract said I had to pay for the first 90 days, whether my father stayed or not. I've talked to a couple of lawyers (a little late, I know). They say the fact that my father couldn't stay the full 90 days because he died is irrelevant. I agreed to pay for 90 days, and so pay for 90 days I must.

Pro-rate what I've had to pay and it comes out to $466 per day for each of the 23 days my father did live there. For $466 a day I could have found a nice hotel room with room service and hired private care. It isn't moral, and it isn't ethical, but it's legal.

— Paulette

■ ■ ■

Lesson learned: Take any residential contract home. Read it slowly and carefully. Twice. If there's something you don't understand, find a professional who understands real estate contracts and elder care issues, and have it reviewed. Have it reviewed even if you think you do understand it. Once signed, it is binding even if something unexpected happens.

- ■ Is there a "trial period" during which a resident can move out without penalty?

    _____

    _____

    _____

- ■ How much notice must be given before a voluntary move out?

    _____

    _____

    _____

- ■ Is there a special form to be completed?

    _____

    _____

    _____

■ If a move is medically necessary, will any required notice be waived?

_____

_____

_____

■ If a move is medically necessary, will any of the charges for the unused part of the month be refunded?

_____

_____

_____

■ If a scheduled move needs to be postponed for any reason, may the resident pay day-to-day for a few extra days? How many?

_____

_____

_____

CHAPTER TWENTY-THREE

Involuntary Discharge

• • •

Mother has Alzheimer's, and she's always been a little hard to get along with. That's why we finally had to move her into the dementia unit in the first place. Recently she started hitting the aides when she didn't want to do something. One day she spit on another resident. She got really sick right after that and had to go to the hospital. When she was ready to come home they said she couldn't come back because she was "dangerous." I know she was a bit of a problem, but aren't they supposed to be trained to take care of people with dementia? No one ever said a word about wanting her out until she went to the hospital.

— Jackson

• • •

Every now and then, an assisted living facility will be unable or unwilling to continue caring for a resident. The marketing representative probably won't spend much time reviewing the possible reasons a resident might be asked to leave. Talking about "failures" isn't a very good sales technique.

However, failures do happen. If you don't want an unpleasant surprise then it is important that you know under what circumstances a resident can be asked to move out, and what steps you might take to minimize the possibility. Make sure you understand completely what they mean by the answers that they give you.

■ What are all of the reasons that a resident could be asked to leave?

_____

_____

_____

■ Under what circumstances might it be necessary to hire private caregivers to avoid being asked to leave?

_____

_____

_____

■ Who makes the final decision?

_____

_____

_____

■ Is there an appeal process? If so, what is it?

_____

_____

_____

- How much notice is given?

  _____

  _____

  _____

- How is notice given, and to whom?

  _____

  _____

  _____

- What will the facility do to help you find an alternative?

  _____

  _____

  _____

- If the facility is discharging a resident, is there a refund?

  _____

  _____

  _____

- What is the process for collecting any refunds of monthly rent, deposits and fees?

  _____

  _____

  _____

CHAPTER TWENTY-FOUR

In Conclusion: Gearing Up for Action

Now that you've . . .

- asked the really important questions
- gotten answers you can live with
- had an attorney read the paperwork over
- adjusted any unrealistic expectations

. . .**NOW** you can go ahead and sign the lease agreement with some confidence.

Keep in mind that there is no assisted living residence on the planet that can give you the answers that you want to hear to every single question you ask. But, if you don't ask, you won't know the situation until it is too late.

The real issue is: are you getting the right answers to the questions that are most important for both you and your elder?

If you are, and you are confident that the person answering your questions knows what he or she is talking about (and has the authority), then move forward.

If you are not, then step back and reconsider. Things probably won't get better over time with this facility or this manager.

Always keep in mind that everything in life is subject to change. Managers leave, staff turnover is inevitable, and facilities are bought and sold all the time. What is perfect today could change for the worse tomorrow. Or, what is less than ideal today may suddenly get a lot better with a change of ownership.

Plan to visit often. When you visit, use your eyes, your ears, your nose, and your common sense to evaluate, and re-evaluate the care your loved one is getting.

If you can't visit as often as you'd like, consider teaming up with a Geriatric Care Manager. A good Geriatric Care Manager can be a lifesaver, especially for families at a distance who want to keep their fingers on the pulse of their eldercare situation.

The Care Manager will visit regularly, work with the facility to resolve any problems, be a friend and "surrogate family" to the resident, and communicate regularly with family members. The Care Manager can even accompany the resident to doctor or other appointments where an accurate exchange of information is important.

If you need to find a Care Manager in your area, the National Association of Professional Geriatric Care Managers has an informative website at www.caremanager.org. You can find a member Care Manager by ZIP code, city and state, or by name.

Be reasonable in your demands, and remember that the staff are human beings, too. They'll respond to compliments and thanks for a job well done.

Best wishes to you and your elder!

Molly Shomer

Training & Education

 These are the training and/or education requirements for Assisted Living Administrators and Direct Care employees in assisted living facilities in each of the United States.

Administrator/Direct Care Employees

State	Administrator	Direct Care Employees
Alabama	6 hours annually	16 core hours on basic first aid, CPR, personal care, infection control, resident rights. Certified Nurse Aides are exempt
Alaska	None specified	None specified
Arizona	21 years of age; 12 months experience; certified	Initial orientation, 12 hours annual training; current CPR

State	Administrator	Direct Care Employees
Arkansas	Current residential care facility administrator certification or complete a prescribed course	Basic orientation & 6 annual hours continuing education
California	Certification including 40 hours classroom training & 20 hours annually	On the job training
Connecticut	10 hours orientation	10 hours orientation. Competency exam & one hour bi-monthly training for aides
Delaware	"Appropriate" training	"Appropriate" training
D.C.	None specified	None specified
Florida	21 years of age, high school graduate or GED, competency exam, 12 hours education every 2 years.	26 hour training & exam. Additional training by job definition.
Hawaii	2 years experience in a health & human services field; completion of administrator's course.	CPR & First aid; 6 hours continuing education

State	Administrator	Direct Care Employees
Idaho	Residential care administrator's license	8 hours orientation & 8 hours annual training
Illinois	Not specified	Not specified
Iowa	"Appropriate to the task"	Unspecified
Kansas	License	Orientation & regular in-services
Louisiana	21 years of age; Bachelor's degree + 2 years' experience or Master's degree	Orientation & annual training
Indiana	License	Nurse Aide training
Maine	State training + 10 hours annual education	State certification
Maryland	"Adequate knowledge"	"Orientation & training"
Massachusetts	21 years of age, Bachelor's degree or equivalent experience. 6 hours annual education.	6 hours orientation, 6 hours annual education
Michigan	1 year experience + 16 hours training	18 years of age + "training"

State	Administrator	Direct Care Employees
Minnesota	Orientation & mandatory training	Competency evaluation
Missouri	H.S. graduate or GED. 6 hours annual education	Orientation & training on state-specified subjects
Montana	H.S. graduate or GED. 6 hours annual education	Orientation & training on state-specified subjects
Nevada	21 year of age. High School graduate + 5 years experience, or Associate's degree + 3 years experience, or Bachelor's degree in health field. 12 hours annual education	"Necessary skills" + 8 hours annual education
New Jersey	Licensed nursing home administrator or pass approved training & exam. 20 hrs additional education every 2 years.	State certification. 10 to 20 hours continuing education every 2 years, depending on classification
New Mexico	"Appropriate to responsibilities"	State certification, in-services

State	Administrator	Direct Care Employees
New York	21 years of age, Master's degree in Social Work + 1 year experience, or Bachelor's degree + 3 years' experience	State-approved training course
North Carolina	21 years of age, state certified	State certified
North Dakota	12 hours annual education	Orientation
Ohio	Licensed nursing home administrator or complete equivalent training	Orientation, training & appropriate competency testing
New Hampshire	12 hours annual continuing education	Orientation, training & in-services
Pennsylvania	40 hours training, 6 hours annual education.	Orientation
Rhode Island	21 years of age. Certified. 16 hours annual education	"As appropriate"
South Carolina	Licensed	Orientation & annual "on-going training"

State	Administrator	Direct Care Employees
South Dakota	High School diploma, 75 hour training program	Formal orientation & ongoing education with required subject matter
Tennessee	Certification	None specified
Texas	Administrators of facilities with 17 + beds must have Associate's degree in nursing, health care mgmt. or related field; Bachelor's degree, or 1 year experience in management or health care	Orientation; 16 hours on-the-job training, 6 hours annual education
Vermont	21 years of age; Experience in gerontology + supervisory & management skills. 15 hours annual training	Orientation & annual training
Washington	21 years of age; High School grad; 2 years experience or degree/certification	Orientation & training
West Virginia	10 hours annual training	Orientation, training & in-services

State	Administrator	Direct Care Employees
Wisconsin	21 years of age; High School graduate; administrative experience or post H.S. training & experience; 45 hours initial training + 12 hours annually	45 hours initial training; 12 hours annual training
Wyoming	Certified nursing assistant or equivalent	As necessary

State Oversight Agencies

 These are the state agencies responsible for monitoring residential care facilities. Contact your state agency for information about what they found on their most recent inspections.

ALABAMA

*Alabama Department
of Public Health*
Box 303017
Montgomery, AL 36130
(334) 206-5075
www.adph.org

ALASKA

Health Facilities Licensing
4730 Business Park Blvd.
Anchorage, AK
(907) 561-8081
www.hss.state.ak.us/dhcs/hflc.htm

ARIZONA

*Arizona Department
of Health Services*
1647 E. Morton Avenue
Phoenix, AZ 85020
(602) 674-4200
www.azdhs.gov/

ARKANSAS

Arkansas Department of Health
5800 W. 10th Street
Little Rock, AR 72204
(501) 661-2165
www.healthyarkansas.com/

CALIFORNIA

California Department of Health Services
1800 3rd Street
Sacramento, CA 94234
(916) 445-3054
www.dhs.ca.gov

COLORADO

Colorado Department of Public Health
4300 Cherry Creek Drive, South
Denver, CO 80222
(303) 692-2819

CONNECTICUT

Connecticut Department of Public Health
410 Capitol Avenue
Hartford, CT 06134
(860) 509-7543
www.dph.state.ct.us/

DELAWARE

Office of Health Facilities Certification
3 Mill Road
Wilmington, DE 19806
(302) 577-6666
www.state.de.us/dhss/index.html

DC

Department of Consumer & Regulatory Affairs
614 H. Street NW
Washington, DC 20001
(202) 727-7780

FLORIDA

Agency for Health Care Administration
2727 Mahan Drive
Tallahassee, FL 32308
(850) 487-2528
www.fdhc.state.fl.us/index.shtml

GEORGIA

Department of Human Resources
2 Peachtree, NW
Atlanta, GA 30303
(404) 657-5700

HAWAII

Hawaii State Department of Health
1270 Queen Emma Street
Honolulu, HI 96813
(808)586-4090
www.hawaii.gov/doh

IDAHO

Idaho Department of Health & Welfare
450 W. State Street
Boise, ID 83720
(208) 334-6626
www.healthandwelfare.idaho.gov

ILLINOIS

llinois Department of Public Health
525 W. Jefferson Street
Springfield, IL 62761
(217) 782-2913
www.idph.state.il.us

INDIANA

*Indiana State
Department of Health*
2 North Meridian Street
Indianapolis, IN 46204
(317) 233-7403
www.in.gov/isdh

IOWA

*Iowa Department of
Inspection & Appeals*
Lucas State Office Building
Des Moines, IA 50319
(515) 281-4233
www.idph.state.ia.us

KANSAS

Kansas Department of Health
900 SW Jackson
Topeka, KS 66612
(913) 296-1240
www.kdhe.state.ks.us/

KENTUCKY

*Kentucky Cabinet
for Human Resources*
275 E. Main Street
Frankfort, KY 40621
(502) 564-2800
www.chfs.ky.gov/

LOUISIANA

*Louisiana Department
of Health & Hospitals*
Box 3767
Baton Rouge, LA 70821
(504) 342-0415
www.dhh.state.la.us

MAINE

*Maine Department
of Human Services*
35 Anthony Avenue
Augusta, ME 04333
(207) 624-5443

MARYLAND

Maryland Department of Health
4201 Patterson Avenue
Baltimore, MD 21215
(410) 764-2750
www.dhmh.state.md.us

MASSACHUSETTS

*Massachusetts Department
of Public Health*
10 West Street
Boston, MA 02111
(617) 727-1299
www.mass.gov/dph

MICHIGAN

*Health Facility Licensing
& Certification*
525 W. Ottawa
Lansing, MI 48909
(517) 241-2637
www.michigan.gov/mdch

MINNESOTA

*Minnesota Department
of Health*
Box 64900
St. Paul, MN 55164
(612) 643-2171
www.health.state.mn.us

MISSISSIPPI

*Mississippi State
Department of Health*
Box 1700
Jackson, MS 39215
(601) 354-7300
www.msdh.state.ms.us/

MISSOURI

Missouri Department of Health
Box 570
Jefferson City, MO 65102
(573) 751-6302
www.health.state.mo.us

MONTANA

*Montana Department
of Health & Human Svcs.*
Box 202951
Helena, MT 59620
(406) 444-2037
www.dphhs.state.mt.us

NEBRASKA

*Nebraska Department
of Health*
Box 95007
Lincoln, NE 68509
(402) 471-4961
www.hhs.state.ne.us/reg/regindex.htm

NEVADA

*Nevada Department
of Human Resources*
1550 E. College Parkway
Carson City, NV 89710
(702) 687-4475

NEW HAMPSHIRE

*Department of Health
& Human Services*
6 Hazen Drive
Concord, NH 03301
(603) 271-4966
www.dhhs.state.nh.us

NEW JERSEY

*New Jersey State
Department of Health*
CN 367
Trenton, NJ 08625
(609) 588-7733
www.state.nj.us/health

NEW MEXICO

*New Mexico Department
of Health*
525 Camino de Los Marquez
Santa Fe, NM 87501
(505) 827-4200
www.health.state.nm.us

NEW YORK

*New York State
Department of Health*
99 Washington Avenue
Albany, NY 11210
(518) 473-1564
www.health.state.ny.us

NORTH CAROLINA

*North Carolina Department
of Human Resources*
Box 29530
Raleigh, NC 27626
(919) 733-7461
www.dhhs.state.nc.us

NORTH DAKOTA

*North Dakota
Department of Health*
600 E. Boulevard Avenue
Bismarck, ND 58505
(701) 328-2352
www.health.state.nd.us

OHIO

Ohio Department of Health
Box 118
Columbus, OH 43266
(614) 466-7857
www.odh.state.oh.us

OKLAHOMA

*Oklahoma State
Department of Health*
1000 NE 10th Street
Oklahoma City, OK 73117
(405) 271-5288

OREGON

Oregon Health Department
Box 14450
Portland, OR 97214
(503) 731-4013

PENNSYLVANIA

*Pennsylvania
Department of Health*
Health & Welfare Building
Harrisburg, PA 17120
(717) 787-8015
www.dsf.health.state.pa.us/health

RHODE ISLAND

*Rhode Island
Department of Health*
3 Capitol Hill
Providence, RI 02908
(401) 222-2566
www.health.ri.gov/

SOUTH CAROLINA

*South Carolina
Department of Health*
2600 Bull Street
Columbia, SC 29201
(803) 737-7205
www.dhhs.state.sc.us

SOUTH DAKOTA

*South Dakota
Department of Health*
615 E. 4th Street
Pierre, SD 57501
(605) 773-3356
www.state.sd.us/doh

TENNESSEE

Tennessee Department of Health
426 5th Avenue North
Nashville, TN 37247
(615) 741-7539
www.state.tn.us/health

TEXAS

*Texas Department
of Human Services*
701 W. 51st Street
Austin, TX
(512) 438-2625
www.tdh.state.tx.us

UTAH

*Division of Health Systems
Improvement*
Box 16990
Salt Lake City, UT 84114
(801) 538-6559
www.health.utah.gov

VERMONT

*Vermont Department
of Aging & Disabilities*
103 South Main Street
Waterbury, VT 05671
(802) 241-2345
www.dad.state.vt.us/lp

WASHINGTON

*Washington Department
of Health Services*
Box 45600
Olympia, WA 98504
(360) 493-2560
www1.dshs.wa.gov/

WEST VIRGINIA

*West Virginia
Department of Health*
1900 Kanawha Boulevard, East
Charleston, WV 25304
(304) 558-0050
www.wvdhhr.org

WISCONSIN

*Wisconsin
Department of Health*
Box 309
Madison, WI 53701
(608) 267-7185

WYOMING

*Wyoming Department
of Health*
First Bank Building
Cheyenne, WY 82002
(307) 777-7121

Glossary of Important Terms

 Every group, business, industry, sport (and so on) has its own special vocabulary. If you can speak a little of the language you will be a whole lot less confused, and a whole lot more powerful in your negotiations.

■   ■   ■

Acute Care
Medical or non-medical care focused on curing disease and rehabilitating the patient

Activities of Daily Living
The basic activities necessary to get through the day: bathing, toileting, grooming, dressing, eating, and transferring (ADLs)

ADL
Shorthand for "Activities of Daily Living"

Administrator
The individual who manages a facility

Adult Day Care
A program in the community where the elderly or the disabled are provided structured activities and services in a protected environment during the day

Adult Foster Care
One or more adults living with an un-related individual or family who provide care and some services

Adult Protective Services
An agency that investigates suspected elder abuse, neglect or exploitation.

Advanced Directives
Legal documents intended to make an individual's health care preferences known. May include Healthcare Power of Attorney (Proxy), Living Will or Do Not Resuscitate Order (DNR)

Aging in Place
Remaining in the chosen living environment as care needs increase

ALF
Assisted Living Facility

Alzheimer's Unit
A living area within an Assisted Living Residence or a Nursing Home designed specifically for the care of individuals with Alzheimer's Disease – often locked to prevent wandering.

Ambulation
The act of walking

Ambulatory
Able to walk

Ambulatory Care
Health care services that do not require an overnight stay and that are provided at a location to which the patient must travel

Assessment
A formal evaluation of physical or mental status

Assisted Living Facility (ALF)
A non-medical residential community offering meals, housekeeping, assistance with activities of daily living, and medication monitoring and assistance - also known as Personal Care Home, Residential Care Home, Board & Care Home.

Board & Care Home
See: Assisted Living Facility

CCRC
See: Continuing Care Retirement Community

Care Management
Professional planning, arranging, monitoring and coordinating care services, either short or long term

Care Manager
A professional who provides Care Management services.

Chronic Care
Medical or non-medical care for a condition with no expectation of great improvement

Cognitive Impairment
A deficiency or reduction in memory, reasoning, orientation or judgment

Companionship Service
Individuals who provide conversation and companionship, but do not provide personal care or housekeeping services

Congregate Housing
Any housing arrangement where multiple individuals live under one roof – most usually refers to Independent Living or Supportive Housing

Conservator
See: Guardian

Continence
The ability to control bowel and bladder

Continuing Care Retirement Community
Housing designed to provide for a range of needs, from independent living through assisted living and skilled nursing care

Continuum of Care
The full range of care, from at home with community resources

through Adult Day Care, Assisted Living and Nursing Home (ex: Continuing Care Retirement Communities provide the full continuum of care)

Convalescent Home
See Nursing Home

Custodial Care
Care focusing primarily on deficits in Activities of Daily Living

Do Not Resuscitate Order
A legal document stating that a patient is not to be resuscitated

DNR
See Do Not Resuscitate Order

Guardian
A person appointed by the court to act on behalf of someone who has been declared incompetent. Sometimes known as Conservator.

Hands-On
Physical assistance with an activity requiring the helper to touch the person receiving assistance.

Home Health Care
Care provided in the home by either unlicensed (Non-Medical Home Care) or licensed (Medical Homecare) providers.

Hospice
Specialized care for the terminally ill focusing on comfort and pain relief

Incontinence
The inability to control bladder and or bowels

Independent Living
Usually multi-unit apartment housing, often providing meals and other supportive services. Residents are functionally independent.

Instrumental Activities of Daily Living
Higher level daily tasks such as cooking, shopping, housekeeping, money management, managing medications.

Living Will
A legal document stating a person's wishes for or against treatment options in the event of a terminal illness.

Medicaid
Jointly-funded federal and state health insurance benefiting elderly and disabled individuals with low income and few resources.

Medical Home Care
Care provided in the patient's home that is supervised by a physician and provided by licensed professionals

Medicare
Federal medical insurance for individuals who are over age 65 or disabled

Medigap Insurance
Private health insurance that covers costs not covered by standard Medicare. Amount of coverage varies by policy.

Non-Ambulatory
Unable to ambulate, or walk

Non-Medical Home Care
Care provided in the patient's home that is non-medical in nature: Custodial care

Nursing Home
A facility that provides 24-hour nursing care. May be called Skilled Nursing Facility or Convalescent Home

Occupational Therapy
Specialized therapy designed to improve the ability to manage Activities of Daily Living (ADLs)

Ombudsman
An impartial advocate for residents of care facilities who is trained to resolve problems and complaints, if possible.

Personal Care Home
See: Assisted Living Facility, Residential Care

Physical Therapy
Specialized therapy designed to improve mobility and strength

Rehabilitation
General term for necessary physical, occupational or speech therapy

Residential Care
Assisted Living, often in a small, "homelike" facility

Respite
Temporary relief for a caregiver. Care may be provided at home or in a facility.

Skilled Nursing Care
Care supervised by a physician and provided under the 24-hour supervision of a Registered Nurse.

Skilled Nursing Facility
See Nursing Home

Stand-By Assistance
Help from a caregiver who remains within reach to prevent a fall. Often involves verbal cueing or reminders of how to do an activity.

Survey
An investigation by the agency responsible for licensing or certifying a facility. Surveys may be routine or in response to a complaint.

Transferring
Moving from one position to another, i.e. from bed to chair or from sitting to standing

About the Author

 For more years than she cares to count Molly Shomer has worked exclusively with seniors and their families, helping them find their way through the "eldercare maze."

"During the time I've been working with aging Americans and their families, I've seen the birth and development of assisted living care. I've watched the industry come of age, and I've walked through the halls of every kind and size of residence. I've talked with hundreds of people who were confused about what it is, about what it can offer, and what it can't. I've helped far too many families relocate elderly loved ones who were in the wrong place because their families didn't know what to look for in advance.

'I've also worked with families who were very happy with the facility they chose, and I've learned from these residences how things *should* be done.

'I've read and re-read dozens of Agreements and Contracts. No two contracts are the same, and no two facilities are identical. "The devil is in the details," as they say. Learning what to look for in an assisted living contract and in the services offered is the key to finding the right place."

Molly maintains a license as a Master's Level Social Worker. The National Association of Professional Geriatric Care Managers recognizes her as a Professional Level GCM. She is also a sought-after consultant and speaker to professionals and organizations concerned with eldercare issues.

Molly's website at *www.eldercareteam.com* offers a broad array of information and resources for elder caregivers and access to the free bimonthly newsletter "Eldercare Matters." You are invited to contact her via email at molly@eldercareteam.com Her telephone number is (972) 395-7823. She welcomes your questions or comments.

AWESOME ENTERTAINMENT
RECORDS

Written by:
Stuart Kallen

Published by Abdo & Daughters, 6535 Cecilia Circle, Edina, Minnesota 55439.

Library bound edition distributed by Rockbottom Books, Pentagon Tower, P.O. Box 36036, Minneapolis, Minnesota 55435.

Library of Congress Number: 91-073054   ISBN: 1-56239-047-3

Cover illustrated by: Terry Boles
Inside Photos by:
    Bettmann News Photo: 9, 18, 23, 29, 31
    Pictorial Parade: 12, 15-16, 21, 26, 28
    Globe Photos: 22

Edited by: Rosemary Wallner

TABLE OF CONTENTS

IMAGINE...

Everyone dreams—even animals. When we dream, we may see and hear things that don't exist. Even when we are awake, we sometimes daydream, and imagine things that aren't there—a ghost, a hot fudge sundae, an image of a place, a song. That is the human imagination at work. If we wanted to, we could draw a picture, write a song, or tell a story about what we saw in our "mind's eye." We could combine images or ideas that have never been put together before. That's creativity. If we show our creative project to friends or family, it usually makes them happy. That's entertainment.

Since everyone dreams, we can be sure that our ancient ancestors were dreamers too. Maybe they considered their night visions to be messages from gods and goddesses—visions of a better hunting ground just over the hill, or a better way to make a tool. It's possible that when these primitive people had a very vivid dream, they scratched images of it in the sand or on a cave wall. From these humble beginnings, art was born.

4

MAGIC CAVE ENGRAVERS

The Pyrenees Mountains form a massive rock barrier between the European countries of Spain and France. About 30,000 years ago, the Pyrenees were teaming with animal life. Reindeer, bison, ibexes, and other animals roamed the rocky crags and green valleys. They were hunted by the ancestors of today's lions and tigers—and by our own ancestors.

The most fantastic images of early human artwork can be found in several caves in the Pyrenees Mountains. The area is rich in iron oxide, a naturally occurring mineral. Around 28,000 years ago, someone turned this substance into vibrant red paint by mixing it with water. They went deep into the caves near Lascaux, France, and began to paint on the rock walls using fine twigs for brushes.

From their hand, a lavish herd of bison, deer, horses, and cattle appear to race wildly across the cave walls and ceilings. Jungle cats, five reindeer swimming across a river, and a wounded bison dying in front of a hunter decorate the walls. Some animals are just charcoal outlines, some are filled with bright earth tones. All show an artist's skill that brings the animals to life 300 centuries after their creation. This incredible gift from the past was discovered by accident in 1940.

When the dirty walls of a dingy cave were transformed into the world's first art museum, neighboring people may have come to inspect the drawings. Suddenly, people had a new place to gather—not to hunt, not to work, but to simply relax and enjoy. As word spread of the new discovery, people might have come from miles around to enjoy the paintings. Other new ideas were exchanged with strangers, and early civilization was formed.

AMAZING ART

Civilization progressed for thousands of years, but the range of the artists' palette remained about the same. Then, around 6,000 B.C., the early Asian people began to discover the artistic possibilities of sap from the acacia tree (called gum Arabic), egg white, gelatin, and beeswax. From this, varnish, enamel paint, and the first colored crayons were made.

As human beings became more civilized and as their towns and cities grew, pottery, jewelry, tapestry, and stained glass became major industries for artists and craftsworkers. Just about every surface in ancient China was lacquered and painted with gold and silver. In 17-century Europe, unpainted wood was considered a sign of poverty, or even worse, bad taste. The paintings made during that time are the most valuable the world has ever seen. From the caves of France to the galleries of New York, artists have been doing their part for civilization for more than 30,000 years.

Hang *This* On Your Wall — The largest painting ever made measured almost 725 feet by 100 feet, or 72,437 square feet—about the size of two football fields. The painting, consisting of brightly colored squares over a huge "smiley" face was painted by students of Robb College in New South Wales, Australia. The canvas was unveiled on May 10, 1990.

In 1846, John Banvard painted a panorama of the Mississippi River on a roll of canvas 12 feet high and one mile long. The painting was stored in a barn on Long Island, New York, and was destroyed in a fire shortly before Banvard's death in 1891.

Lend Me Your Ear — The most money ever paid for a painting is $82.5 million for *Portrait of Doctor Gachet* by Vincent van Gogh. The painting was put up for auction on May 15, 1990, and was sold to a Japanese businessman within three minutes. Weeks before van Gogh made the painting of his doctor, he had cut off his ear and mailed it to a woman he loved. Shortly after, madness drove van Gogh to suicide. In 1989, van Gogh's *Irises* sold for $53.9 million, a record at the time. Van Gogh might appreciate the fact that five of his paintings are considered the most valuable in the world. When he was alive, van Gogh never sold one painting!

The painting that is considered the most valuable in the world is the *Mona Lisa,* painted by Leonardo da Vinci, which hangs in the Louvre Museum in Paris, France. Painted between 1503 and 1507, the painting is considered to be worth over $500 million.

*Portrait of Dr. Gachet
by Vincent van Gogh.*

*The Mona Lisa, painted by
Leonardo da Vinci.*

9

Paint It Again Bill — William Bixler of Anderson, Indiana, reproduced his painting, *"The Old Swimmin' Hole,"* over 5,000 times between 1912 and 1918. This gives Bixler the world's record for the most repetitious painter.

That's Crazy! — The largest sculpture in the world (it is still being carved) will be that of the Oglala Indian chief known as Crazy Horse. The sculpture was begun on June 3, 1948, on a mountainside near Mount Rushmore, South Dakota. Carving Crazy Horse on horseback into the mountain was the life's work of Korczak Ziolkowski, who died in 1982. Since his death, his children and friends have continued his work. When done, the sculpture will be 563 feet high and 641 feet long. The horse's nostril alone is 50 feet deep and 35 feet across.

STUPENDOUS STAGE AND SCREEN

Long before movies, radio, television, and Broadway plays, early humanity enjoyed musical theater. Primitive men and women celebrated harvests, births, deaths, and victories over enemies with music and dance. What is thought to be the earliest document of musical theater is painted on a cave wall near Ariege, France. The painting, dating to 10,000 B.C., shows a man wearing a buffalo mask, playing a stringed instrument, and dancing wildly behind a herd of reindeer. This man might have been a magician insuring a good hunt.

The ancient Greeks elevated theater to a high form about 600 B.C. The Greeks employed professional actors and musicians to perform tragedies, comedies, and mime.

What a Circus — About 2,100 years ago, the Romans brought theatrics to new heights (and depths) with the Circus Maximus. Like today's circus, the Circus Maximus boasted several death-defying acts. The only difference was that in those days, death was not defied so much as guaranteed. The first circus offered deadly chariot races and battles between men and beasts. During one season, 2,000 gladiators and 230 wild animals were killed. During a 13-year stretch, over 3,500 lions and tigers and quite a few gladiators were killed. Later Roman circuses seated up to 150,000 people who came to watch races, bet, drink wine, and eat food.

Circus Maximus in Rome about 2,100 years ago.

THE SILVER SCREEN

The opera, ballet, and theater that existed for hundreds of years was pushed into the 20th century with the invention of motion pictures. The first motion picture ever made was filmed by Louis Prince in Washington Heights, New York, in 1885. Thomas Edison patented movie film in 1891. The movie film was actually invented by his assistant William Dickson, but Edison took the credit (and the money). Edison opened the world's first movie studio in 1893. He opened the first movie theater in New York City on April 14, 1894. For five cents, a customer could watch a short film strip of a body-builder lifting weights or Buffalo Bill shooting his pistols. The "peep-show" theater was a huge success. Movie stars, special effects, and a multi-billion-dollar industry were not far behind.

Big Bucks For Bad Blood — Arnold Schwarzenegger's movie *Terminator 2: Judgement Day* is the most expensive movie ever made. Loaded with special effects, the action-adventure film cost about $90 million to produce. The previous most expensive movies were 1990's *Total Recall* and *Die Hard 2* which cost about $70 million each.

Cleopatra, starring Elizabeth Taylor and Richard Burton was made in 1963 at a cost of $44 million, which would translate into $176.5 million at 1990 rates. Taylor changed costumes 65 times during the course of the movie, setting a record.

Bring Your Own Popcorn — The longest film ever made was Werner Fassbinder's *Berlin Alexanderplatz,* which was shown in Hollywood, California, in 1983. The movie was 15 hours and 21 minutes long and included a two-hour break for dinner.

Alien Nation — Americans love movies about outer space and aliens enough to make them the highest earning films in United States history. *E.T. The Extra-Terrestrial* has earned $228 million since 1982, setting the world's record. The second most watched movie was *Star Wars,* which has earned $193 million. Third place goes to *Return of the Jedi,* which grossed $168 million.

In 1989, total box office receipts in the United States and Canada totaled over $5 billion, the highest in history. Eight films earned over $100 million, another record. The film *Batman* broke a record by earning $40.5 million in its first three days. Jack Nicholson, who played "The Joker" in *Batman* was paid $60 million for the role, setting the record for the highest paid actor.

E.T. has earned a record $228 million.

Jack Nicholson, who played "The Joker" in Batman was paid $60 million for the role.

Elementary My Dear Watson — The character of detective Sherlock Holmes has been portrayed in more movies than any other. The super-sleuth Holmes has been played by 70 actors in 197 films between 1900 and 1988.

In horror films, the character of Count Dracula has been represented 155 times. His closest rival, Frankenstein, has been played 109 times.

*The character of Count Dracula
has been represented 155 times.*

16

A Set to End All Sets — The largest movie set ever built was for the film *The Fall of the Roman Empire* in 1964. It was built on 55 acres near Madrid, Spain. The set took 1,000 workers seven months to build 22,000 feet of stairways, 601 columns, 350 statues, and 27 full-size buildings. The Roman Forum was built out of 170,000 cement blocks.

It Makes You Want to Screen — The largest movie theater in the world is Radio City Music Hall in New York City. Opened in 1932, the theater seats 5,874 people.

The tiny European country of San Marino has one movie theater for every 3,190 residents, giving it more movie theaters per person than any other country. The United States has one movie theater for every 11,000 people. Saudi Arabia is the only country with no movie theaters. Public presentation of movies is illegal there because of strict religious beliefs.

The country with the most movie-going people is China. In 1988, over 21 billion movie tickets were sold. That equals 21 tickets per person.

The outside of Radio City Music Hall.

The inside of Radio City Music Hall has 6,200 seats. This is the largest theatre in the world.

TELEVISION

Television could have existed almost 50 years before it became a reality. The basic principles for it were being developed independently in Germany, England, Scotland, France, Russia, and the United States. Unfortunately, the pioneers of television did not know about each other, and some ideas were beyond the technology available at the time. Maybe if they could have seen each other on television...

On October 2, 1925, John Baird of London, England, transmitted the image of a ventriloquist's dummy onto the first television set about 10 feet away. Since then, thousands of dummies have been projected onto millions of television screens all over the world.

There's No Vision Like Television — The first television broadcasts in the United States were in 1928. These broadcasts were only watched by researchers who reported splitting headaches and severe eyestrain. With the development of a superior tube, the first public broadcast was by the Radio Corporation of America (RCA) on July 21, 1931, in New York City. By 1940, there were 23 television stations in the United States.

By 1949, there were over one million TV sets in America; by 1951, over ten million. By 1959, the United States counted over 50 million television sets. In 1990, over 500 million homes worldwide had TV sets. The United States leads the world with 90.4 million sets, 80.9 million of which are color sets. Fifty-one million Americans watch cable TV, and 54 million homes have more than one set.

American Couch Potatoes — Americans watch more television than anyone else. Between the ages of two and 11, the average child watches about 32 hours of TV a week. It has been reported that the average American child sees at least 12,000 acts of violence on television every year. They also see 26,000 murders on television before their 18th birthday.

The Whole World Is Watching — The global audience for the 1990 World Cup tennis finals, played in Italy from June 8 to July 8, was estimated at 26.5 billion people. The total number of people tuning in the XXIII Olympic Games in Los Angeles, California, between July 27 and August 13, 1984, was about 25 billion. Since there are only five billion people in the world, many millions of people must have watched every day.

Sylvester Stallone as "Rambo."

The largest audience for a single broadcast was 1.6 billion for the Live Aid concerts, on July 13, 1985. Dozens of bands played music in Philadelphia, Pennsylvania, and London, England, for the benefit to aid starving children. Live Aid was shown in 140 countries and transmitted by a record 12 satellites. Nearly one-third of the world's population watched the show.

The "Muppet Show" is the most widely viewed program in the world with an audience of 235 million in 106 countries. The final episode of "M*A*S*H" is the most widely viewed single program. When it aired on February 28, 1983, 60.3 percent of all households, or 125 million people in the United States, tuned in.

Kermit sings a song in a scene from "The Muppets at Disney World."

Pudding Your Money Where Your Mouth Is

— Television star Bill Cosby is currently the highest paid performer on TV, having earned $92 million during 1987 and 1988. This includes his weekly show, concerts, albums, endorsements, and pudding commercials.

Bill Cosby during a concert at Radio City Music Hall.

Huge Tube — The Sony Jumbo Tron TV screen is the largest in the world. The screen measures 80 feet by 150 feet. The set was displayed at a Tokyo, Japan, trade show in March 1989.

Tiny Tube — The Seiko TV-Wrist Watch has a 1.2-inch screen and weighs 2.8 ounces. The smallest color television is the LCD Japanese Epson with dimensions of 3 inches by 6.75 inches by 1.12 inches. The entire set weighs almost one pound.

MAGICAL MUSICAL TOUR

Human beings probably made music even before they invented language. Primitive people struck sticks together to frighten away wild animals. In time these "clappers" were used rhythmically along with work songs in the field to ease the burden of labor. Drums and flutes made of animal bone were used over 25,000 years ago in dance rituals to please the gods and insure a good harvest.

While it is impossible to find the exact roots, the beginning of organized music can be traced to the cradle of civilization, Mesopotamia (present-day Iraq). Between 3500 and 500 B.C., the people who lived in this area left remains of every basic type of musical instrument: idiophones, triangle-like instruments with a loud clang; aerophones, flute-like instruments that respond to blown air; cordophones, harp-like instruments with strings; and membranophones, drum-like instruments made from animal skins and gourds.

For thousands of years, humanity has listened to the music of tribal and religious chants, wandering minstrels, opera, and classical music. When Thomas Edison invented the record player in 1877, music came out of the churches and concert halls and into everyone's living room. With the coming of radio during the 1910s, music became a daily part of everybody's life. African-American musicians combined the rhythmic music of Africa with spirituals and modern instruments to give us blues, jazz, boogie-woogie, and good old rock 'n roll.

Star Guitars — The largest playable guitar in the world is 19 feet tall and was constructed by the Narrandera Country Music Association in 1989.

The most money ever paid for a guitar was $288,000 in 1990 for the Fender Stratocaster that belonged to legendary rock guitarist Jimi Hendrix.

Jimi Hendrix

Bang the Drums — The largest drum ever made is 13 feet across and was played in the Royal Festival Hall in London, England, on May 31, 1987.

26

The largest drum set in the world consists of 81 pieces and belongs to Darreld MacKenzie of Alberta, Canada. The drum set has 45 drums, including six bass drums, 15 cymbals, five wood blocks, two triangles, two gongs, two sets of wind chimes, six cowbells, a vibra slap, and an icebell.

You Say It's Your Birthday — The most frequently sung song in the English language is *"Happy Birthday to You"* written by Kentucky Sunday school teachers Mildred Hill and Patty Hill in 1893. The song was sung by the Apollo IX astronauts from outer space on March 8, 1969.

They Must Have a Big Dressing Room — On July 17, 1872, Johann Strauss conducted an orchestra of 987 pieces and a choir of 20,000 at the World Peace Jubilee in Boston, Massachusetts. There were 400 violins playing in the world's largest orchestra.

Can You Play "Far Far Away?" — On April 17, 1982, 6,179 "musicians" gathered at Bay Port Mall in Milwaukee, Wisconsin, to play "Stars and Stripes Forever" by John Phillip Sousa. According to one music critic, the instruments included kazoos, soda bottles, coffee cans, bongo drums, and anything else a person could thump on. "At times," the critic said, "you could almost tell what they were playing."

Beatle Hits — John Lennon and Paul McCartney, from the supergroup The Beatles, have co-written more number-one singles than anyone else. McCartney is credited with 32 number-one hits and John Lennon is credited with 26. They wrote 23 number-one hits together. The most successful female songwriter is Carole King with eight number-one songs.

Paul McCartney and John Lennon.

Richest Man in the Mirror — Michael Jackson holds several world's records in the entertainment industry. Jackson was already the highest paid singer in the world earning an average $92 million a year, when he signed a $1 billion contract with

Sony in 1991, by far the largest contract ever signed by an entertainer. Two other records that Jackson holds include being paid $11.9 million for four soft-drink commercials and selling out seven nights in a row at Wembley Stadium in England in August 1988. At Wembley, 504,000 people saw Jackson perform live in one week—no other performer can make that claim. The total gross of Jackson's 1987-1989 world tour brought in a record $124 million. Jackson's album *Thriller* has sold 40 million copies, more than any other single album ever made.

A Rolling Stone Gathers Money — The Rolling Stones' *Steel Wheels* concert tour that ended in December 1989, is the most successful concert tour ever. The Stones played to over 3.2 million people in 30 cities and grossed more than $310 million.

Say What? — Daddy Freddy of London, England, is said to be the world's fastest rapper. On November 24, 1989, Daddy Freddy rapped 507 syllables in one minute. This would break down to 200 to 250 words in one minute, or three to four words per second.

Mick Jagger and Ron Wood of the Rolling Stones.

STICKS AND ROCKS TO ROCK 'N' ROLL

Art and music has come a long way since our distant relatives lived in caves. Or has it? Does the same primitive instinct that moved our ancestors continue to move us when we see a beautiful painting? When we hear the beat of music, does some long-forgotten part of our soul remember distant rhythms? It must be, because of the high value art and music still have in today's fast-forward society. So remember, it's the creativity in all of us that has pushed the human race from the animal chase to outer space.